MEET OUR SAGES

Meet Our Sages

BY JACOB NEUSNER

BEHRMAN HOUSE, INC.
PUBLISHERS

ACKNOWLEDGMENTS

My thanks go to those who shared in making this book: Alan J. Peck and Martin Jaffee, assistants; Samuel, Eli, and Noam Neusner, and Rabbi Joel Zaiman, readers; Linda Altshuler, copy-editor; David Altshuler, coordinating editor; Kathy Jungjohann, designer; and Seymour Rossel, friend and encourager. B. Barry Levy and Emanuel White took full charge of the Hebrew text.

J.N.

Library of Congress Cataloging in Publication Data
Neusner, Jacob, 1932–
   Meet our sages.

   1. Tannaim—Juvenile literature. 2. Aggada—Juvenile literature I. Hellmuth, Jim.
II. Title.
BM501.2.N48   296.6′1   80-12771   ISBN 0-87441-327-3

© 1980 by Jacob Neusner
Published by Behrman House, Inc., 235 Watchung Ave., West Orange, N.J. 07052
Designed by Kathy Jungjohann
Illustrated by Jim Hellmuth
Manufactured in the United States of America

For good neighbors and good friends

Henry Berger
Samuel and Hella Flescher
Eric and Anne Flescher
Jonathan and Ruthie Tepper
Joel Flescher

PREFACE

"Our sages of blessed memory (חֲכָמֵינוּ זְכרוֹנָם לִבְרָכָה)" are rabbis of ancient times, from the first through the sixth centuries of the Common Era. The sages created the Mishnah and the Talmuds and many other holy books. These books, all together, are the "oral Torah" (תּוֹרָה שֶׁבְּעַל-פֶּה).

Judaism is the religion of two Torahs, the written one that Moses received at Sinai and wrote down, and the oral one that Moses received at Sinai but did not write down. (Later, great rabbis wrote down the oral Torah in the Mishnah and the Talmuds and other holy books.) These two Torahs together are the one whole Torah of Moses, our rabbi. When we speak of "Judaism," we mean the one "whole Torah of Moses, our rabbi."

This book and the two that follow it are meant to introduce you to the oral Torah: first, to the ancient sages who formed it; second, to the Mishnah, its principal part; and third, to the Talmud, which explains the Mishnah. In this book we meet sages as people. We ask what is a sage, how does a person become a sage, what does a sage do, and how does a sage think. We answer these questions by studying carefully five stories told about sages. In the two later books, *Learn Mishnah* and *Learn Talmud,* we go on to study the words of sages, things they actually said and thought. In all three books we ask how these words speak to us and what they mean for us today.

I have to add a special word to the young women who will read this book. Our sages in ancient times were nearly all men. Often, I shall speak of "he," referring only to the men who are under discussion. I do not exclude women from the discussion, where women are present. But that is mainly in the setting of issues of our own day. I believe that the sages have much to teach Jewish women, as they do Jewish men. Now it is for the young Jewish women of our own day to take up the work of Torah and to become learned in ways in which their mothers and grandmothers, in general, were not.

I dedicate this book to my neighbors who also are family to us, beloved friends for my wife and myself and for our four children. Hella Flescher's father, Mr. Henry Berger, is like a grandfather to all of us, and we sit near one another in *shul* every week. Hella Flescher and Samuel Flescher, and their children, are very dear to our family. We are happy and lucky to have such good friends as our neighbors.

J.N.

Contents

PART ONE

Who Are Our Sages?

1. Who Are Our Sages?

The sages are men who learn so much Torah that they themselves become Torahs. What they do *is* Torah. They are people who do things *naturally* in the way in which the Torah, given by God, wants us to do things. Sages are important not only because they learned a great deal and teach us important truths. Sages are important because the way they lived in their day—two thousand years ago—still is a model of the holy way of life, the way in which we should live. Their teachings teach us.

So when we meet our sages—men who lived two thousand years ago and whose teachings the Mishnah and the Talmud give to us—we meet people we may copy. You know that there are people worth following, and people not worth following. Among your friends are some whom you admire, and some whom you do not think are so smart. So when you meet the wise men of the Mishnah and the Talmud, you meet people who teach by example as much as by what they say. Your teachers, parents and rabbis are supposed to be good examples for you. But sages always are good examples.

The sages were wise men. There were few women among them, although women in olden times in the Land of Israel did become wise too. But in those days it was not common for women to be given an important place. Nowadays things are different and better. Women have good reason to become wise and to study Torah. They have a greater share than they used to in the life of the Jewish people. They have much more to say. So women nowadays frequently study Torah. Like their brothers, they go to Hebrew schools, Sunday schools, *yeshivot*, colleges and universities. Their minds matter. This is one important way in which things are better now than they once were.

But in many ways things do not change. The sages of the early centuries of the Common Era understand and explain things that do not change. What, after all, do sages really know? They teach lessons about kindness and patience. These are things we need to learn. Sages talk about Torah and the meaning of the life of the Jewish people under the rules of Torah (Part One and Two). These things tell us who we are and what we should become. They tell us we can be better than we are. They talk about how to overcome

problems, even terrible calamities, in the life of the Jewish people (Part Three). Unhappily, these are not foreign to us. Sages debate among themselves about questions which go on and on (Parts Four and Five). We may join in their debates because these questions face us as much as they faced the sages.

We call these men not merely "sages" but "*our* sages" because they are wise particularly in the Torah, which makes us who we are and makes us like the sages. And the Torah is what makes the men, women, and children of your temple or synagogue and your community into *Israel*, into the Jewish people. Our sages are "our thing," like the Torah, which makes us different from everyone else in the world. The sages are our sages because they belong to us, and we to them. They belong to us not because their teachings are merely interesting, or only smart; their teachings are Torah as much as "In the beginning, God created the heaven and the earth" is Torah. Their teachings come from Heaven, as much as "You shall not murder" comes from Heaven.

That is the point of the first story we shall study together, a story in which someone asks for "the whole Torah," and the sage does not *even* bother to repeat a verse taken from the written Torah.

We have covered many important ideas in these few pages. First, let us list them. Then we shall try to unpack them and find a way to turn them into our own words, our own ideas. These questions will help.

1. **What is a sage? What makes a person into a sage?**
2. **What is the Torah? Have you ever seen a Torah? Can a person be a Torah?**
3. **Who is a model for you?**

4. What is a "way of life"? Do you live in a certain "way of life"?

5. What is a holy way of life? What makes something holy?

6. When did sages live? Is it important that they lived a long time ago? Where did they live? Does that make any difference?

7. Can a woman be a sage? Are there wise women in your Jewish community? Do they hold important positions and do interesting things?

8. What are questions important to you, which sages might answer for you?

9. Why is it important that sages are "our sages"? How do their teachings help us to understand what is a Jew, and what a Jew is supposed to do?

10. How can something be "Torah" which is not written in the books of Moses, the prophets, or the writings—the Tanakh, that is, the Hebrew Scriptures or the Bible?

2. How Do We Meet Our Sages?

The stories about our sages are short and complete. You will be surprised at how carefully they are told. Every word matters. Every phrase is in place.

Where do we find these stories?

They are found, whole and complete, just as you will read them, in the books that the sages of olden times wrote. These books are the Mishnah, the Talmud, and other collections of the third, fourth, and fifth centuries of the Common Era.

These books begin with the Mishnah, a vast account of how things are supposed to be in Israel, the Jewish people. The Mishnah tells, specifically, about how life is to be lived at home and in the synagogue, in the family and in the streets. It explains how the whole life of the Jewish people is supposed to be organized.

Since the Mishnah is such a large and important book, it was quickly made the subject of study. As a result, important explanations for the Mishnah and expansions of its teachings came into being. These explanations and expansions of the Mishnah, along with the Mishnah itself, were made into the Talmud.

In fact, two groups of people studied the Mishnah, and each one made a Talmud for itself.

One group was in the Land of Israel, and they made the Mishnah and their comments into the Talmud Yerushalmi, the Talmud of Jerusalem, which also is called the Palestinian Talmud.

The other group was in Babylonia—the land that is present-day Iraq. They made a still more important and interesting Talmud around the Mishnah. This is called Talmud Bavli, the Babylonian Talmud. When people refer to "the Talmud" without further explanation, they mean the Babylonian Talmud.

The Mishnah contains a special section (or "tractate") called Abot, which contains teachings about what we should do every day. A kind of "Talmud," called "The Fathers according to Rabbi Nathan," was created for Abot. That "Talmud" tractate contains many stories about the sages who give sayings in Mishnah-tractate Abot. In fact, to the people who made

"The Fathers according to Rabbi Nathan," it is important that the men who say things in Mishnah-tractate Abot also be *real* people. That is, they wanted to tell stories about the people who stand behind the sayings. They tell who they were and give them flesh, bones, and blood. They do not think a saying without a face is worthwhile.

Now all of the stories we study have one thing in common. They all are important because they say important things. They are not important because they really happened on one particular day, for one particular reason. In fact, if they tell about something that happened only once, they are not important. These stories are supposed to tell us about truths that apply every day, forever. Sages do not believe that one day is more important than another, or that one happening means more than some other.

So keep in mind that the issue is not, Did this story really happen the way the storyteller says it happened? The issue is, Is this story true for me? Is it really true for the Jewish people? Does it describe how the Jewish community should be? Does it contain a lesson important for us now? If the answers to those questions are yes—and you are the one to decide that—then the stories are true. They are true because they make sense today. And if they are not true, it is not because they did not happen, but because we do not think they should *ever* happen.

How are we going to learn the stories, to meet our sages?

Our plan is simple.

First, we shall ask what questions we want a story to answer. I shall spell out for you what I think the really important matter is.

Second, we shall read the story, line by line, to be sure we understand all of its parts.

Sometimes a story may require explanation, which I shall give you. But the main thing is that we understand the story in every detail, in every word. That way you will gain the skills to read stories on your own.

Third, we shall stand back and read the story from beginning to end, so that we do not lose sight of the story as a whole.

Fourth, we shall discuss the meaning of the story. We shall ask whether it really does answer the question that I ask at the beginning.

Finally, we shall try to draw out of the story the important truth for ourselves.

This is our plan. It should make sure you grasp the parts and the whole, the trees and the forest. In the end you should have learned new words. But

you also should have discovered a new way of thinking about things.

If you do, you will want to learn not only stories about people. You will want to know how to make sense of the holy books, the Mishnah and the Talmud, which present these stories and teach truth in other ways besides telling stories.

The goal of this way of learning the stories, of meeting our sages, is to show you why Jewish men and women over the ages have studied, and continue to study, the Mishnah and the Talmud. You will learn why they found it worthwhile to learn these particular books. You will discover what they found in them.

So let us begin by meeting our sages.

1. **Do all stories tell just what happened one day? When you ask, "Is it really true?" do you always mean, "Did it really happen?"**

2. **How does a story make an important point? Can you think of an example of a story that you have heard?**

3. Did George Washington really chop down the cherry tree? Is that the point of the story? Would you want to see the stump of the cherry tree? Why not?

4. Can you think of a document that tells how things are supposed to be in America or in Canada? What are the sorts of books or documents that tell us how life is to be organized?

5. Why do you think such a book or document will require more study? Is it easy to apply to life today the teachings of a book written ten years ago?

6. Why would people want to continue to apply the teachings of an old book to the life of the present day?

7. Why do you think it was important for the sages of the Land of Israel and of Babylonia to work separately to explain the Mishnah? Why do you think they also had to cooperate and share the work?

8. Why did the people who told stories about the rabbis of Mishnah-tractate Abot ("The Fathers") think it urgent to tell such stories? Why was the saying not enough?

9. When we ask, "Is this story really true?" how shall we know the answer? Where shall we look for the measure of the truth?

10. Why is it important to examine each story line by line? Why is it important to stand back and to see the story as a whole? What do we learn from the details? What are we supposed to see in the story as a whole?

3. The Sage and Torah

HILLEL, SHAMMAI, AND THE PERSON WHO WANTED TO LEARN TORAH
Babylonian Talmud Shabbat 31a

The word "Torah" appears in nearly every line of this book. Until now, we have not said what we mean by "Torah." This story will tell us. But the meaning is not the one we expect.

You know what a Torah (or, the Torah) looks like. In your synagogue there is a place—an ark, or aron— in which the Torah is kept. Yet I called the sage a kind of Torah. So, obviously, there is some other meaning for "Torah" besides, "A scroll that is kept in the holy ark and taken out and read in the synagogue on the Sabbath."

That "scroll that is kept . . . ," as you know, contains the Five Books of Moses, the written Torah.

There is another meaning of Torah. "Torah" can refer to a living person, a person who has Torah to teach. It is not merely a person who can cite what is in the written Torah, or who can explain what Moses means when he says something in the written Torah.

It is this other sense of "Torah," this "living Torah," that comes out of the story we shall now study.

In this story, somebody asks a sage to teach "the whole Torah."

But that is not the only thing you will find surprising in the story.

The amazing thing is that the man asks for "the whole Torah" while he stands on one foot.

Clearly, he does not leave much time for the recitation of the five books of Moses, from Genesis through Exodus, Leviticus and Numbers, and down on into Deuteronomy. He wants something else: he wants to be told the point of it all. That is not a simple request.

Finally, what is astounding is that the answer he receives is not even in "the Torah," not in the Five Books of Moses.

We shall come back to these problems when we have learned the story in its entirety.

20

BABYLONIAN TALMUD SHABBAT 31a

A certain gentile came before Shammai	נָכְרִי אֶחָד בָּא לִפְנֵי שַׁמַּאי
[and] said to him,	אָמַר לוֹ:
"Convert me	גַּיְּירֵנִי
"on condition that you teach me the whole Torah	עַל מְנָת שֶׁתְּלַמְּדֵנִי כָּל הַתּוֹרָה כּוּלָּהּ
"while I stand on one foot."	כְּשֶׁאֲנִי עוֹמֵד עַל רֶגֶל אַחַת
He pushed him out with the builder's cubit which was in his hand.	דְּחָפוֹ בְּאַמַּת הַבִּנְיָן שֶׁבְּיָדוֹ.
[When] he went before Hillel,	בָּא לִפְנֵי הִלֵּל
He converted him [as]	גַּיְּירֵיהּ
he said to him,	אָמַר לוֹ:
"What is hateful to you,	דַּעֲלָךְ סְנֵי

21

"do not do to your neighbor.
"That is the whole Torah,
"and the rest is commentary;
"go and learn [it]."

לַחַבְרָךְ לָא תַּעֲבֵיד
זוֹ הִיא כָּל הַתּוֹרָה כּוּלָה,
וְאִידָךְ - פֵּירוּשָׁהּ הוּא,
זִיל גְּמוֹר.

Vocabulary

gentile	נָכְרִי	hateful	סְנֵי
convert me	גַּיְירֵנִי	your neighbor	חַבְרָךְ
on condition	עַל מְנָת	do	תַּעֲבֵיד
you teach me	תְּלַמְּדֵנִי	the rest	אִידָךְ
the whole	כּוּלָה	commentary	פֵּירוּשׁ
pushed him out	דְּחָפוֹ	go	זִיל
builder's cubit	אַמַּת הַבִּנְיָן	learn	גְּמוֹר
to you	עֲלָךְ		

4. How the Story Works

When you look at the story, you see that it is told by drawing a striking contrast. The contrast is simple and easy to see. It is between Shammai and Hillel. Shammai is impatient and Hillel is patient. Shammai cannot answer the question at all. Hillel has an answer to the question.

But there is a second important side. The whole story is made up so as to highlight Hillel's answer to the question. The response is surprising because it answers an unanswerable question—how to repeat the whole Torah while standing on one foot!

Without the story, the saying would be striking: *What is hateful to you do not do to someone else.* But with the story, the saying becomes the centerpiece of a little play, a drama.

There are, in fact, three units to the story:

(1) Impatient Shammai

(2) Patient Hillel

(3) What Hillel said: What is hateful . . .

When you see things this way, you realize that nothing is by accident. Everything is planned.

The storyteller, in fact, is a kind of artist. The art is in the simplicity of the story. Anyone can understand the main point. If it looks smooth and easy, the reason is that the artist is skillful and careful. The hardest thing of all is to make things look easy and obvious.

But the saying will never be easy or obvious. For what Hillel says is that we have to do to other people only things that we could accept for ourselves. We must not do things we do not want others to do to us. That means Hillel provides us with a general rule to govern all of the everyday bruises and bumps that people give one another. It is not easy or obvious to make up one rule for all those different events. But Hillel did it—and the storyteller makes it look easy and obvious.

1. **Can a word have more than one meaning? Can it refer to more than one thing? What words mean more than one thing? What words mean more than they say?**

2. How is Torah able to refer to more than one thing? What are some of the meanings attached to that word?

3. Why does a Torah occupy the center of the synagogue? What do we say when we give the Torah pride of place?

4. Can a person be a thing? Why do we say that a person can be a "living Torah"?

5. Why is Shammai right in turning away the one who wants the whole Torah while standing on one foot? Does Shammai say something important through his gesture?

6. Why does the storyteller not tell us that Hillel was kind to the person and answered his question? Why does the storyteller jump right to the point? What did Hillel have in his hand?

7. Why does Hillel claim that his "golden rule" covers the whole Torah? Does he mean to say that nothing else matters? If that is not what he means, then what is in his mind?

8. Why is it important to the storyteller to lay matters out as carefully as he does? What are some of the marks of careful work?

9. If the saying of Hillel is not even in Hebrew—is not in the written Torah—then how can it be Torah?

10. If a saying that is not in the Torah is Torah, then what is Torah? What makes the saying Torah at all? Does the storyteller want to make a special point in using that saying as the centerpiece of the story?

<table>
<tr><td>

5.
The
Boundaries
of Torah

</td><td>

First of all, let us reread the story of Hillel, Shammai, and the person who wanted to learn Torah, so that we can see it as a whole. Then we shall discuss it as a whole.

</td></tr>
</table>

BABYLONIAN TALMUD SHABBAT 31a

נָכְרִי אֶחָד בָּא לִפְנֵי שַׁמַּאי, אָמַר לוֹ: גַּיְּירֵנִי
עַל מְנָת שֶׁתְּלַמְּדֵנִי כָּל הַתּוֹרָה כּוּלָהּ כְּשֶׁאֲנִי עוֹמֵד עַל רֶגֶל אַחַת.
דְּחָפוֹ בְּאַמַּת הַבִּנְיָן שֶׁבְּיָדוֹ. בָּא לִפְנֵי הִלֵּל, גַּיְּירֵיהּ. אָמַר לוֹ:
דַּעֲלָךְ סְנֵי לְחַבְרָךְ לָא תַּעֲבֵיד — זוֹ הִיא כָּל הַתּוֹרָה כּוּלָהּ, וְאִידָךְ —
פֵּירוּשַׁהּ הוּא, זִיל גְּמוֹר.

. . . A certain gentile came before Shammai [and] said to him, "Convert me on condition that you teach me the whole Torah while I stand on one foot." He pushed him out with the builder's cubit which was in his hand. [When] he went before Hillel, he converted him [as] he said to him, "What is hateful to you, do not do to your neighbor. That is the whole Torah, and the rest is commentary; go and learn [it]."

The first thing we notice when we read the whole story is that it is remarkably short. The author tells us little. He does not give any details that we do not need to know to grasp the main point. He does not tell us, for example, the day of the week or where Shammai was standing. If he was at work ("with the builder's cubit in his hand"), then perhaps he was impatient because he did not have time. But that is the main point: there is no time.

Why did the person who asked come at all? And if he came to learn the Torah, why was it for so brief a time? Was that the real purpose? The storyteller does not say. He wants *you* to ask those questions and draw your own conclusions. He makes you ask questions by not answering the questions to begin with.

Finally, why does the storyteller not tell us what he thinks of someone who treats "the Torah" so lightly as to say, "I'll take it, if you make it easy"? Perhaps he would have been wiser to ridicule the question, rather than answering it.

The storytellers, whose work we shall study here, believe in painting with only a few broad strokes. They want to suggest many things by saying only a few things. They leave room for your imagination. They think that the person who hears the story can be trusted to see its points. So they believe you are smart people. Their basic idea is that the people to whom they tell stories really know the stories already.

And that brings us to the main point, the notion of Torah as something we already know.

Hillel's answer is striking because it is obvious, plain, undecorated. It says the simplest thing in the simplest way. And it is in the language people spoke every day. If the story were told today in America or Canada, it would be told in Hebrew, but the "punchline" would be in English. That would be odd, so it would make you sit up and take notice.

So Torah is simple and obvious, and it is in the language of everyday speech—whatever that language is.

Here is the main point of the story: Torah is not something in books only. Torah also is in the streets. Torah is (1) something you discover in life. It is (2) something you find in books that you also find in life. And it is (3) something you find in everyday events that you also find in books.

From our viewpoint, what is most important is that in this story Torah has a meaning that we should never have predicted. Torah with a small t—*torah*—is something we find in the world. It is a truth we learn in the world.

So what is Torah as this story tells it?

Torah is a truth so perfect and appropriate, that it sums up in a handful

of words everything worth knowing. It is not enough to say, "Torah is true." It is misleading to say, "Torah is truth." For not all truth is Torah. And when we say, "Torah is true," we have not said enough.

The point of the story is that there is Torah to be learned from someone who lived more than a thousand years after Moses. Therefore, there is Torah to be learned from someone of our own day, from one of our sages.

And behind that statement is something not said: that *act* of giving the Torah, which took place long ago at Sinai, goes on and on. The Torah is given not only on one day, at Sinai. The Torah is given every day, and Sinai is everywhere. The Torah is given not only to one man, Moses. The Torah is given to everybody who learns Torah. The Torah is given not only in one place, however holy, but everywhere and in every language. So the Torah is given every day, and the people of Israel, the Jewish community, comes into being every day *when it receives Torah.*

Part of that Torah we receive is the written Torah, the five books of Moses, which are written on the Torah-scrolls and carefully preserved in the holy ark in the synagogue.

And part of that Torah is not written in the Torah but is preserved in the record of the teachings and the doings of our sages, the sages whom we remember, and the sages whose memory is a blessing for us—so we call them *our sages of blessed memory.*

There are two Torahs, the written one and the unwritten one. What is not written down in Scripture is given in the lives and teachings of those people, after Moses, through whom the Torah of Moses passed onward, down to us.

All of this in a little story, of three sentences? Yes and no. Some of it is there, all of it is necessary to make sense of what is there.

So if people become living Torahs, if what they say and do is *torah,* then we have to ask, How do they get that way? How does someone become a sage? The next story is going to answer that question.

1. Why do we pay attention to *how* someone tells a story, as well as to the story itself? What do we learn?
2. How does the storyteller choose what to tell us, and what not to tell us?
3. Why does the storyteller give us so little information? What is the plan in telling us less than we need to know? Can you think of other ways in which to stimulate your imagination?
4. Why does the story give the principal Torah-saying in the speech of everyday people? Do you think Hillel could have said the saying in a language (Hebrew) that the man did not know?
5. What other point is made by having the story said in everyday language, rather than in Hebrew? Is there a message here about the character of torah? About the meaning of Torah?
6. When we say, torah is in the streets, what do we mean? Does God care about what happens only in the synagogue?
7. How are we going to recognize torah in the streets? Will we find torah in the way in which people act toward one another? Will we find in the Torah important rules about how people should act to one another?

8. Why does Hillel teach that the most important thing is how we act toward one another?

9. Why does Hillel maintain that to find out what not to do to someone else, we must figure out what we would not want someone to do to us?

10. Is there an advantage in phrasing matters in a negative way? Is there an advantage in saying, "What you want others to do to you, do to them"? What are the advantages of each way of saying the same thing? Or are they really the same thing?

PART TWO

How Do You Become a Sage?

6. How Do You Become a Sage?

It is natural for a Jew to carry out the teachings of the Torah. That is a difficult idea. It means that, without really trying, we live in an ordinary way just as the Torah teaches. We are happy when the Torah thinks we should be happy, on the Sabbath or on a festival. We are sad when the Torah thinks we should be sad, for instance, when we recall the unhappy events of the history of the Jewish people. Our good traits are the qualities the Torah teaches, such as kindness to other people and honesty. Our bad qualities—and we all have bad qualities, it's human nature—are things that the Torah helps us to overcome.

When we talk about a person who is a living Torah, therefore, we talk about someone who is a model for us all. We learn Torah from such a person's actions.

But how does someone make himself or herself over in such a way as to become a "living Torah" or a sage, one of "our sages of blessed memory"?

Naturally, in the writings of the ancient sages people will tell stories to answer that question. The reason is that they have to explain to themselves who they are and how they got to be the way they are.

Before hearing the answers, let us try to imagine for ourselves possible answers to these questions.

First, does it not seem reasonable that the stories will be about children who are five or six years old? After all, if you become a sage through studying Torah, then you probably begin at a young age.

Second, does it not seem likely that the stories will praise the parents of the little child who is going to become a sage? After all, they are the ones who brought the child to the school for classes.

Third, should we not expect the story to tell us something about what the child learned in school? If the child studies Torah, then what is the subject to be studied? Should we not know that the child learned this book of the Bible or that tractate of the Mishnah?

These are the kinds of questions you might expect to be answered when you are told how a sage becomes a sage.

But they are not the kinds of questions the storyteller wants to answer.

He has a different set of questions. They are much more difficult.

First, he wants to know what the parents of a future sage think about their child's becoming a sage. This is an amazing question because we should take for granted the mother and father will be happy. But that is not so.

Second, he wants to make sure we know that the sage becomes a sage because of a decision of his own. It is *not* natural. It is not normal. Above all, it is not something someone else has decided for him.

Third, the storyteller stresses that becoming a sage is difficult. It means you live without much food, without a good roof over your head, because you are not earning a living and have little money. It means you are hungry much of the time.

Fourth, the storyteller wants to emphasize the love of the teacher for the student. The teacher does not merely teach facts. The teacher teaches concern by showing that he cares for the student. The teacher by example teaches important lessons. The storyteller tells us that fact by not mentioning any of the lessons the teacher teaches the student, but only by speaking about things the teacher does for the student.

Finally, we shall see something familiar. The real point of the story will come in a saying.

You recall that at the climax of the story about Hillel and Shammai is the famous saying of Hillel's. Clearly, the storyteller has made things up in such a way that that saying stands at the top of the hill. So we may say that one thing these sorts of stories will want to give us is an explanation of some famous saying, attached to the name of a given sage.

One famous saying attached to the name of Hillel is, "What is hateful to yourself do not do to someone else." The story provides the saying with a dramatic setting.

So the saying stands out still more because it is really out of place in its setting.

When we come to the famous saying in the story before us, we find something odd and personal. The saying has to do with—of all things—bad breath! The reason this particular sage had bad breath is explained. It is made into a Torah-saying.

When you hear things about ancient sages, you expect to hear about how wise or how good they were. But in this story, you do not hear humble things, not even nice things. We do not expect to hear a story about how a sage of old had bad breath or needed to take a bath, was short or tall or had pimply skin. We always assume that to be a sage you have to look like a movie star.

But that is not a belief in Judaism. Torah thinks that a person who becomes a sage is not necessarily someone who is born so beautiful, or who smells so nice, or who has such smooth skin, or is of such ideal height and weight, that to all eyes that person obviously is a sage. Being a sage is something you make of yourself.

This brings us back to where we started: to the idea that it is *natural* to be a living Torah. It is not natural that we are born into the Torah. Being a sage, looking like a sage, is unnatural. Our inborn traits have nothing to do with it.

What is natural is not natural: You learn to be a sage. But, when you do learn, you discover in your heart and mind and soul that it is natural to be what you have become. You make yourself into what you are.

That sounds like a paradox. But if you are a pre-teen, you know that it is the simple truth. You are at an age of making decisions and then discovering that the decisions are right for you, natural to what you really are. You are discovering yourself.

It is hard to discover yourself. It is hard to be yourself—to be your best, your most natural self. That is why the stories about sages are interesting. They show us how sages learned to become what they truly were meant to be.

In the stories about the sages, you see people discovering what they really are.

1. What do we mean when we talk about "doing what comes naturally"? What are the sorts of experiences that seem natural to us? Do we ever use "it's natural" as an excuse?

2. What do the sages mean when they speak of what is natural? Is this the same sort of thing that we mean?

3. What do we mean when we say that a person is a living Torah and carries out the teachings and gives an example of the Torah?

4. What does the Bible mean when it says that human beings are made in the image of God, that Adam and Eve—the first man and the first woman—are in the image of God?

5. Does this have anything to do with the idea of living by the Torah as "doing what comes naturally"?

6. Why do you think a storyteller will have to tell us about the origins of a sage? Do you think the storyteller also will have to tell about other points in a sage's life?

7. What are the sorts of stories you expect, and what are the kinds you do not expect? What is the difference?

8. If it is difficult to become a sage, and if even the sages' parents do not nurture their child to become a sage, then how can it be natural to become a "living Torah"?

9. Do you think a "famous saying" became attached to a sage because of something the sage really did or said? Or do you think the sage was famous before the saying became famous?

10. Why do you think that sages are not represented as physically beautiful or unblemished people? Why did that fact not matter to people? What do you think really mattered to people who admired and respected a sage?

7. The Beginnings of a Sage

ELIEZER BEN HYRCANUS GOES TO STUDY TORAH
Abot d'Rabbi Nathan
Chapter Six

liezer ben Hyrcanus was one of the leading sages toward the end of the first century of the Common Era (from about 50 to about 120 C.E.). His master, Yohanan ben Zakkai, was the head of that entire generation of sages. In the story after this one, we shall see Yohanan ben Zakkai with Eliezer ben Hyrcanus at the most critical moment in the history of the Jewish people of that age. So Eliezer went to study with a truly great man.

Eliezer himself became great. What is great about Eliezer ben Hyrcanus is that he shared in the work of the rebuilding of Judaism after the destruction of the Second Temple in 70 C.E. He was one of that small group of sages who made it possible for Torah to go forward, even without the Temple, and for the Jews to find in Torah the reason to go forward.

There are two amazing things in this story of the origins of Eliezer ben Hyrcanus.

First, his father did not want him to become a sage.

Second, the story does not tell us what Eliezer learned to become a sage.

As we noticed in the last chapter, these are surely the two things any story about the beginnings of a sage should tell us: first, that the sage's parents had a part in it, and second, that the sage's teacher taught him some specific things.

In this story we see that becoming a sage is an act of decision on the part of a mature person. It is as if you decide, when you go to college, that you want to become a veterinarian or to work for the government or to become an engineer or an architect. It is your decision, not your parents' decision.

Your parents may approve it. They may not. But you have to make that decision, and no one can make it for you. That, the story tells us, is the way to become a sage: Only you can decide.

But the amazing thing is that, after all is said and done, no one in the story tells us the contents of the Torah Eliezer learned from Yohanan ben

Zakkai. Rather, the story wants to make sense of a "famous saying" attached to the name of Eliezer ben Hyrcanus. Indeed, it looks as though the story begins with the saying and goes on from there.

You know how stories spin out. They make important points and then raise questions that bring up still more important points. So stories grow.

Now let us learn the story in its entirety.

ABOT D'RABBI NATHAN CHAPTER 6

What was the beginning of
  Rabbi Eliezer ben Hyrcanus?
He was twenty-two years old
and had not [yet] studied
  Torah.
One time he said,
"I will go and study Torah
  from Rabban Yohanan ben
  Zakkai."
Said his father Hyrcanus to
  him,
"You will not taste a thing
"before you plow the entire
  furrow."
He rose early in the morning
and plowed the entire furrow
  [and then went to
  Jerusalem].
He went and sat before
  Rabban Yohanan ben Zakkai
  in Jerusalem,
until a bad breath came out of
  his mouth.
Said Rabban Yohanan ben
  Zakkai to him,
"Eliezer, my son, have you
  eaten at all today?"

מֶה הָיָה תְחִלָּתוֹ שֶׁל
רַבִּי אֱלִיעֶזֶר בֶּן הוּרְקָנוֹס
בֶּן עֶשְׂרִים וּשְׁתַּיִם שָׁנָה הָיָה
וְלֹא לָמַד תּוֹרָה

פַּעַם אַחַת אָמַר
אֵלֵךְ וְאֶלְמֹד תּוֹרָה לִפְנֵי
רַבָּן יוֹחָנָן בֶּן זַכַּאי

אָמַר לוֹ אָבִיו הוּרְקָנוֹס

אִי אַתָּה טוֹעֵם
עַד שֶׁתַּחֲרוֹשׁ מְלֹא מַעֲנָה

הִשְׁכִּים
וְחָרַשׁ מְלֹא מַעֲנָה

הָלַךְ וְיָשַׁב לוֹ לִפְנֵי רַבָּן
יוֹחָנָן בֶּן זַכַּאי בִּירוּשָׁלַיִם

עַד שֶׁיָּצָא רֵיחַ רַע מִפִּיו

אָמַר לוֹ רַבָּן יוֹחָנָן בֶּן זַכַּאי

אֱלִיעֶזֶר בְּנִי כְּלוּם סָעַדְתָּ
הַיּוֹם

He was silent.

[Rabban Yohanan ben Zakkai] asked him again.

Again he was silent.

[Rabban Yohanan ben Zakkai] sent for the owners of his hostel and asked them,

"Did Eliezer have anything to eat in your place?"

They replied, "We thought he would eat with you, Rabbi."

He said to them,

"And I thought he would eat with you!

"You and I, between us, [almost] destroyed Rabbi Eliezer.

[Rabban Yohanan ben Zakkai] said to him, "Even as a bad breath came out of your mouth, so shall your fame go forth in Torah."

שָׁתַק
שׁוּב אָמַר לוֹ

וְשָׁתַק
שָׁלַח וְקָרָא לְאַכְסַנְיָא שֶׁלוֹ
אָמַר לָהֶם

כְּלוּם סָעַד אֱלִיעֶזֶר אֶצְלְכֶם

אָמְרוּ לוֹ אָמַרְנוּ שֶׁמָּא
אֵצֶל רַבִּי הָיָה סוֹעֵד
אָמַר לָהֶם
אַף אֲנִי אָמַרְתִּי שֶׁמָּא
אֶצְלְכֶם הָיָה סוֹעֵד
בֵּינִי וּבֵינֵיכֶם אִבַּדְנוּ אֶת
רַבִּי אֱלִיעֶזֶר מִן הָאֶמְצַע

אָמַר לוֹ כְּשֵׁם
שֶׁיָּצָא לְךָ רֵיחַ רַע מִפִּיךָ
כָּךְ יֵצֵא לְךָ שֵׁם טוֹב כַּתּוֹרָה

Vocabulary

beginning	תְּחִלָּה	again	שׁוּב
twenty-two	עֶשְׂרִים וּשְׁתַּיִם	sent	שָׁלַח
time	פַּעַם	called for	קָרָא
taste	טוֹעֵם	hostel	אַכְסַנְיָא
plow	תַּחֲרוֹשׁ	in your place	אֶצְלְכֶם
entire	מְלֹא	ate	סָעַד
furrow	מַעֲנָה	destroy	אִבַּדְנוּ
rose early in the morning	הִשְׁכִּים	just as	כְּשֵׁם
		your mouth	פִּיךָ
came out	יָצָא	so	כָּךְ
breath	רֵיחַ	fame	שֵׁם טוֹב
was silent	שָׁתַק		

39

8. How the Story Works

The story consists of two parts. Each one is complete in itself. Later, we shall see that each is incomplete without the other. One part tells us how Eliezer ben Hyrcanus went off to study Torah. He was a mature man when he decided to go. His father told him that he could not go until he had done his work. He did the work, and then he went.

The second story is not quite so simple. It wants to explain the famous saying, "Even as bad breath rose from your mouth, so shall your fame travel for your knowledge of Torah."

The two stories fit together. The first one explains why Eliezer had no money with which to buy food; his father sent him off hungry. The first story leads to the second. But each story makes sense without the other.

Once more we look in vain for many details. In fact, the storyteller magically conjures pictures before our eyes, drawn with the fewest and the simplest strokes. He tells us nothing we do not need to know, and he tells us everything we do need to know. It is an amazing artistic accomplishment.

He tells us (1) Eliezer was an adult and had not studied Torah. He does not tell us what Eliezer did all those years.

He tells us (2) Eliezer decided on his own to go and study Torah. He does not tell us why he made that decision. What was lacking in his life?

He tells us (3) Eliezer's father said Eliezer would not eat until he ploughed. That does not explain anything. Yet it gives us a great deal of information. The father does not seem to be a loving and caring parent. He will not feed his adult son until the son does his work. He does not even refer to his son's intention to go away from home.

The climax of the story is striking. Eliezer got up early and did what his father told him. *Then* he went to Jerusalem. (That is a fact we have to supply ourselves.)

This story is strange since it does not make an obvious point. And yet it is a powerful story because in four or five sentences, it conveys a picture of a whole world.

The story shows that the sage leaves a world, in which he grew up, of farmers and workers of the Land of Israel. These people did not think that a

person must leave the fields or the shops to study Torah.

So a sage is someone who decides things on his (and, in our day, *her*) own. He is not a person who accepts things as they are.

Yet the sage-to-be is confronted with the choice of whether or not to violate the Torah by going off to study Torah.

For the Torah teaches, "Honor your father and your mother."

Is it an act of honor to do what a father says? It is indeed. So Eliezer honors his father. But he also honors himself by doing what he has decided to do. That is a profound point.

The other story is longer but simpler. We already know that the story is told so as to lead to its stunning climax, the famous saying.

People are distinguished for different qualities, some thought desirable, some not. Since he was starving, Eliezer had bad breath. That is turned into a good thing. People notice when you have bad breath. Likewise, they will notice you for your learning.

The one thing to take to heart is that the sage wants to be known. You want his teachings to be heard. It is not enough to be a living Torah. You want to be a living Torah among other people. That is why it is a compliment to say that you will be famous someday for your learning, just as you are now famous for having bad breath.

This balances one thing against the other, to show how the effort, or the pain, is related to the reward. Eliezer must live in poverty and starve himself since he has no one to take care of him while he studies. But there will be a reward, not of riches but of fame of a specific sort.

But there is another hero in this story, and we should not lose sight of him. It is Yohanan ben Zakkai, the teacher. He is not the principal actor in the story. Eliezer is. But he is the one who makes the story happen. If Yohanan had not understood, Eliezer would not have become a great sage. So the story really takes place because the teacher was understanding.

1. In what ways is this story different from the one about Hillel and Shammai? Do you think the story about Eliezer is told better than the other one? What are the strengths of this story? Do you find it *interesting*?

2. Can you make up a story about your own beginnings as a student of the Torah?

3. What are the things the storyteller forgets to tell us? Why does he not tell us that Eliezer was a clever student? Why does he not tell us what Eliezer studied?

4. Does the storyteller think we should know who Yohanan ben Zakkai is? Why does he not tell us about Yohanan at all?

5. Why does Eliezer's father not praise him when he tells his father he wants to go to study Torah? What does Eliezer's father want him to do? Why does he want him to do it?

6. Why does Eliezer want to go to study Torah? What does he lack at home? Why does Eliezer obey his father and plough the furrow? Why does he then leave for Jerusalem?

7. Why does Yohanan ben Zakkai care whether or not Eliezer has eaten? Does Yohanan ben Zakkai take responsibility for Eliezer's welfare? Do your teachers ask you how you feel? Does Yohanan ben Zakkai take up the responsibilities that used to belong to Eliezer's father? Does he become a new father?

8. Did your parents receive a good Jewish education? If not, why do they want you to have a good Jewish education? Are they like Eliezer's father, or are they like Yohanan ben Zakkai? Which is the truer father to Eliezer?

9. Why does Yohanan think it is a reward and a compliment to Eliezer to tell him that someday he will be famous? What sort of fame does Eliezer want?

10. Do you think Eliezer's father was happy when his son became famous? Would that change his mind about Eliezer's leaving him and going to Jerusalem?

9. The Boundaries of Torah

First, let us reread the story of the beginnings of Eliezer ben Hyrcanus, so that we can see it as a whole. Then we shall discuss it as a whole.

ABOT D'RABBI NATHAN CHAPTER 6

מֶה הָיָה תְחִלָּתוֹ שֶׁל רַבִּי אֱלִיעֶזֶר בֶּן הוּרְקָנוֹס. בֶּן עֶשְׂרִים וּשְׁתַּיִם שָׁנָה הָיָה וְלֹא לָמַד תּוֹרָה. פַּעַם אַחַת אָמַר אֵלֵךְ וְאֶלְמוֹד תּוֹרָה לִפְנֵי רַבָּן יוֹחָנָן בֶּן זַכַּאי. אָ"ל אָבִיו הוּרְקָנוֹס אִי אַתָּה טוֹעֵם עַד שֶׁתַּחֲרוֹשׁ מְלֹא מַעֲנָה. הִשְׁכִּים וְחָרַשׁ מְלֹא מַעֲנָה. הָלַךְ וְיָשַׁב לוֹ לִפְנֵי רַבָּן יוֹחָנָן בֶּן זַכַּאי בִּירוּשָׁלַיִם עַד שֶׁיָּצָא רֵיחַ רַע מִפִּיו. אָמַר לוֹ רַבָּן יוֹחָנָן בֶּן זַכַּאי אֱלִיעֶזֶר בְּנִי כְּלוּם סָעַדְתָּ הַיּוֹם. שָׁתַק. שׁוּב אָמַר לוֹ וְשָׁתַק. שָׁלַח וְקָרָא לְאַכְסַנְיָא שֶׁלּוֹ אָ"ל כְּלוּם סָעַד אֱלִיעֶזֶר אֶצְלְכֶם. אָמְרוּ לוֹ אָמַרְנוּ שֶׁמָּא אֵצֶל רַבִּי הָיָה סוֹעֵד. אָמַר לָהֶם אַף אֲנִי אָמַרְתִּי שֶׁמָּא אֶצְלְכֶם הָיָה סוֹעֵד בֵּינִי וּבֵינֵיכֶם אָבַדְנוּ אֶת רַבִּי אֱלִיעֶזֶר מִן הָאֶמְצַע. אָ"ל כְּשֵׁם שֶׁיָּצָא לְךָ רֵיחַ רַע מִפִּיךְ כָּךְ יֵצֵא לְךָ שֵׁם טוֹב בַּתּוֹרָה.

What was the beginning of Rabbi Eliezer ben Hyrcanus? He was twenty-two years old and had not [yet] studied Torah. One time he said, "I will go and study Torah from Rabban Yohanan ben Zakkai." Said his father Hyrcanus to him, "You will not taste a thing before you plow the entire furrow." He rose early in the morning and plowed the entire furrow [and then went to Jerusalem]. He went and sat before Rabban Yohanan ben Zakkai in Jerusalem, until a bad breath came out of his mouth. Said Rabban Yohanan ben Zakkai to him, "Eliezer, my son, have you eaten at all today?" He was silent. [Rabban Yohanan ben Zakkai] asked him again. Again he was silent. [Rabban Yohanan ben Zakkai] sent for the owners of his hostel and asked them, "Did Eliezer have anything to eat in your place?" They replied, "We thought he would eat with you, Rabbi."

He said to them, "And I thought he would eat with you! You and I, between us, [almost] destroyed Rabbi Eliezer." [Rabban Yohanan ben Zakkai] said to him, "Even as a bad breath came out of your mouth, so shall your fame go forth in Torah."

The first thing we notice when we read the whole story is that the storyteller takes a number of important things for granted. Some of them are obvious, and some are not.

The storyteller assumes we know who Eliezer ben Hyrcanus is. He takes for granted that we want to know how he started on his way to become a great sage. So the storyteller knows that throughout the Mishnah and the later writings of the Talmudic rabbis, Eliezer is an important name. That is obvious.

What to him is not obvious is what is most striking to us. We have the idea that the Jews of olden times were all great masters of the Bible. We take for granted that during the time in which the Mishnah and the Talmud were taking shape, all Jews wanted to be part of the work, or, at least, respected the ones who did the work.

We assume this because in our own time Jews encourage their children to go to religious school, Hebrew school, Sunday school, or day school and yeshiva. Jews generally agree that they want their children to be learned in Torah. They generally know that to be learned and a good Jew means to study Torah.

But in the time of Eliezer, so far as this story is concerned, things were not that way. In fact, the first story explains how Eliezer was able to obey the Torah's law—"honor your father"—even while he was going to leave his father. So the sage-to-be had the problem of changing his way of life from the way of his parent to the way of Torah.

Nowadays, it is common for children to be more observant than their parents. It is not unusual for children, and not the parents, to keep Shabbat and kashrut. So we know people who are in the situation of Eliezer and who have to do what he did.

But the difference seems to be Eliezer's family did not honor him for his learning. He had to leave his family in order to become a sage.

There are two other basic points. When the young man begins to become a sage, he gives up one father and gets another.

There is one father who will not feed him. So he finds another father, who worries about his having food.

There is one father who makes the food into the reward for ploughing the furrow. There is the other father who makes the Torah the reward for not having food at all.

So there are opposites brought together. The contrast is between the natural father and the father, the great master, who teaches Torah. To be a sage is to find such a master. A sage is never called a sage. He is called a *disciple* of a sage.

And the reason is that learning Torah stands for a boundary. It separates son from father. Study of Torah changes Eliezer and takes him from the field and his family.

Torah brings him to a place where he is only a guest. Torah gives him a father who is only a teacher—a sage, to whom Eliezer is a disciple. So there is no natural path that goes from Eliezer's home to his school.

Your parents lead you from home to school. But for Eliezer going to school means leaving home. It means that he has to make a decision about who he wants to be. He has to decide what he wants to make of himself— against the wishes of his father, who brought him into the world (these stories rarely tell us about the mothers). Studying Torah for Eliezer means a new way of being a person—a new home that is not a home and a new father who is not a father but only a teacher.

When we see matters this way, we understand that the two stories really are one. The storyteller tells the two parts and shows how one is different from the other.

He tells us that studying Torah is not merely gaining facts or information. Studying Torah is a new way of living.

Studying the Torah moves us from one sort of being to another. Just as Eliezer had to leave what he was and become something new in order to study Torah, so anyone today who wishes to become a Jew has to become something new.

That is so even if you grow up in a good Jewish home. For the real point of it all is that to become a student of Torah, you have to make up your own

mind. You have to make the Torah your own. And you do this by taking command of your own life.

1. Why does the storyteller choose to tell a story about some-one who is famous? What is the point of his asking about Eliezer's beginnings?

2. Do you think the Jews during the time of the storyteller all believed in what the sages had to say and accepted their leadership?

3. What is the importance of the storyteller's emphasis on the contrast between the old father and the new teacher? Why does he draw it so carefully?

4. Why is the law, "Honor your father," going to be a problem for the sage-to-be in the time of the storyteller? Do you think that this was a pressing issue? What makes you think so?

5. Why does the storyteller draw a contrast between plough-

ing the field and studying the Torah? If people study the Torah, how will they make a living for themselves and their family?

6. Why is "a sage" always "a disciple of a sage?" Who is the Master of all masters, to whom every "disciple of a sage" in fact serves as a disciple?

7. Why does study of Torah turn Eliezer into something he was not before? Does studying Torah in your school make you into a different person? Should it make you a different person?

8. Why do people have to decide what they want to be? Is it not enough that they are just like their parents? Why make a decision at all?

9. What reward do you think Eliezer would have as a result of the painful decisions he made? Do you think this is enough to pay him back for his suffering? What do you think made him realize that he had to make a decision at all?

10. Why does Torah draw lines? What does it wall in? What does it wall out? Why does the sage stand for boundaries for the Torah? How can a human being serve as a boundary-line?

PART THREE

What Do Sages Do?

10. What Do Sages Do?

Sages learn Torah and live by its teachings. They live the way Moses, our rabbi, wants people to live. Their lives make the teachings of the whole Torah of Moses real and concrete. This much is clear.

So what? What difference does it make to the Jewish people, the community of Israel, that there are sages within the community? Sages are good people who do good things, but are they good for the Jews as a group?

Sages hope to show people how to do things. They want to impress *other* people with the right way and the wrong way. They do not live for themselves. They live for the community as a whole.

You remember how the storyteller made it clear that, in his view, the Jews in general are not sages or disciples of sages. That is why a person like Eliezer had to reject his father and his brothers. He went to a master, who was a new father, a new source of food.

So sages look out onto the community and understand that there are people who are not like them. People do not live like sages and are not disciples of sages. But sages do not turn their backs on that community, which is not like them. They reach out to the community. They hope to lead the community. They are wise, and they know what is good for the Jews, as a community, and what is bad.

Sages lived in the Land of Israel. In their time, colossal events changed the course of the history of the Jewish people in their Land. There were two tremendous moments, much like shocks of our own day: for example, the Holocaust, the 6-Day War, and the Yom Kippur War.

First, early in 70 C.E. the Romans destroyed the Temple that had been built in Jerusalem around 500 B.C.E. The Temple had been the center of the Jews' religious and national life. It had been there that the Jews believed that they worshipped God just as the Torah had said they should. The destruction brought on a tremendous crisis.

Second, less than seventy years later, in 132-135 C.E., the Jews of the Land of Israel raised a revolt against Rome. They did so, many people think, because three generations had passed since the destruction of the Temple. People believed it was time to rebuild the Temple. People remembered that when the first Temple had been destroyed, in 586 B.C.E., seventy years passed until God forgave the Jews. They returned to Zion, regained Jerusalem, and rebuilt the Temple. So now many people expected the same thing to happen.

But that is not what happened. In fact, the opposite happened. While the Jews fought bravely, they lost the war. The Romans then made a law that the Jews could not even go into Jerusalem again. Not only could they not rebuild the Temple, they even lost access to the Holy City. It was not until five hundred years later, after the Moslems conquered the Land of Israel (which they called Palestine), that Jews could go back to the place where the Temple had stood.

You see, therefore, that the Jewish people faced serious problems during the time of our sages of the Mishnah and the Talmud. You understand how much the wisdom of the sages was needed, how much people required their leadership.

For the one thing you must have when everything goes wrong is someone with clear vision. At that time, because the sage understood the Torah, he could explain to people what had happened. He could tell people what they had to do, so that they could go onward, even after the terrible disasters of their own day.

Now what the sage has to say, the leadership he has to offer, is not quite what you would expect.

A leader is someone who tells people what to do. He takes a position of authority. He uses it to guide people and govern them. He takes responsibility. He has the power to carry out his responsibility.

But in the early centuries of the common era, the sages did not hold a position of power. They wanted to govern. In time to come, they did. That is why for many centuries rabbis, that is, sages, were the real leaders of the Jewish people, the judges and decision-makers. But in the time of the Temple's destruction, the sages were not yet in positions of authority. But the sages were respected. They were admired. Their wisdom was acknowledged.

So they had something we should call "moral authority." That is to say, people *listened* to sages because they admired and respected them, not because they had to listen to them. The sages did not have the power to push people around. They had the strength to persuade people through example and teaching.

The message of sages when the Temple was destroyed is just as unusual

as the position from which sages gave their message.

What sages said was that there were still important deeds to be done, holy deeds, even though the Temple was no more. Sages did not say that the Temple had never mattered. They certainly did not rejoice that it had been destroyed.

They mourned for the Temple's destruction, which is why we observe the ninth of Ab (Tisha b'Ab). They prayed for the Temple's rebuilding. That is why we have many prayers that ask for the rebuilding of the Temple, the restoration of the priests to the altar, the offering up, once more, of animal sacrifices, and all the other things that used to be done in the Temple.

The sages said that even though the Temple is lost, all is not yet lost. What goes forward, beyond the destruction of the Temple, is what we shall want to see in this next story.

The sages came up with something to do for people who used to go to the Temple. They were not helpless. They were not hopeless. The reason is that they believed in the Torah. They found in the Torah all of the things the Jewish people needed to know in their time of crisis. So learning in Torah brings people to leadership because they know what to do.

1. Why is it important to ask what the sages do for the community at large? Why is it not enough for sages to be good people and to live a good life?
2. Why is the community important to the sages? Would it not have been enough for the sages to go off and start little private villages or communities of their own?
3. Why do sages want to tell people who are not part of their group the right way and the wrong way?
4. Why do the sages believe the Jewish people as a whole is important? Where do they find the message that Israel, the people as a whole, must be the focus of their teaching of Torah? Who is their model, and whom did they teach?
5. Do you think the example of Moses, whom the sages called "our rabbi," explains why the Torah of the sages was turned into the Torah of Israel, the whole Jewish people?
6. Why did the Jewish people hope that the Second Temple would be rebuilt seventy years after its destruction? Did they find this idea in the Torah?
7. Why was the war fought seventy years after the destruction of the Temple more painful to lose than the first revolt itself? What had changed in the aftermath of the second revolt?
8. What made the sages believe that the people should listen to them in the age of calamity? Why do you think people did listen to them?
9. What do you think the sages believed would continue after the destruction of the Temple? Do you think that they were right?
10. What is the meaning of "moral authority"? Do you know people to whom others listen not because they have to, but because they want to?

11. The Sage and the Emperor-to-be

YOHANAN BEN ZAKKAI GOES TO VESPASIAN AND SAVES THE TORAH
Abot d'Rabbi Nathan
Chapter Four

Vespasian was a Roman general. When the Jews of the Land of Israel rebelled against Roman rule, in the year 66 C.E., the Romans sent a big army to put down the rebellion. Vespasian was the head of the army. First of all, he put down the revolt in the outlying regions, in Galilee, then on the coast. Finally he moved against Jerusalem.

Vespasian was a smart man. He spread his army around Jerusalem and laid siege to the city. He made the choice to wait and to see what would happen. He had two good reasons not to attack Jerusalem right away.

The first reason was that the Jews were not united. Some of the Jews favored the war. Others feared that the Temple would be destroyed if the war went on. So they wanted to surrender to Rome and accept Roman rule. Vespasian had every reason to let the Jews grow weak by fighting one another.

The second reason was that, back in the city of Rome, the Romans were not united either. There were a number of different men who wanted to become emperor of Rome. Vespasian had many friends in Rome and in other parts of the Roman empire. But things were uncertain. No one knew just what would happen. So to Vespasian, it was better to stay in the Land of Israel and fight a war as a hero than to go back to Rome and take a position—which might be a wrong and surely a dangerous position—in the difficult politics of that time. Later, as his opponents eliminated themselves one by one, Vespasian would be in a position to take over and make himself emperor. That is just what he did.

Now the story of how the great sage, Yohanan ben Zakkai, came to the emperor-to-be, Vespasian, and made a deal with him, takes account of these facts. But the important point in the story is not to go over Vespasian's plans or even the policies of Yohanan ben Zakkai. We shall have to find out for ourselves just what points the storyteller really wants to make for us.

This story is longer than the ones we have read up to now. But it is smooth and does not have many hard words. You should be able to read it without much difficulty.

ABOT D'RABBI NATHAN CHAPTER FOUR

When Vespasian came to destroy Jerusalem	כְּשֶׁבָּא אַסְפַּסְיָינוּס לְהַחֲרִיב אֶת יְרוּשָׁלַיִם
he said to them [the inhabitants],	אָמַר לָהֶם
"Fools, why do you seek to destroy this city,	שׁוֹטִים מִפְּנֵי מָה אַתֶּם מְבַקְשִׁים לְהַחֲרִיב אֶת הָעִיר הַזֹּאת
"and why do you seek to burn the Temple?	וְאַתֶּם מְבַקְשִׁים לִשְׂרוֹף אֶת בֵּית הַמִּקְדָּשׁ
"For what do I ask of you	כִּי מָה אֲנִי מְבַקֵּשׁ מִכֶּם
"but that you send me one bow or one arrow,	אֶלָּא שֶׁתִּשְׁגְּרוּ לִי קֶשֶׁת אַחַת אוֹ חֵץ אַחַת
"and I shall leave you?"	וְאֵלֵךְ לִי מִכֶּם.
They said to him,	אָמְרוּ לוֹ
"Even as we went forth against the first two who were here before thee and slew them,	כְּשֵׁם שֶׁיָּצָאנוּ עַל שְׁנַיִם רִאשׁוֹנִים שֶׁהֵם לְפָנֶיךָ וַהֲרַגְנוּם
"so shall we go forth against thee and slay thee."	כָּךְ נֵצֵא לְפָנֶיךָ וְנַהַרְגֶךָ
When Rabban Yohanan ben Zakkai heard this,	כֵּיוָן שֶׁשָּׁמַע רַבָּן יוֹחָנָן בֶּן זַכַּאי
he sent for the men of Jerusalem and said to them,	שָׁלַח לְאַנְשֵׁי יְרוּשָׁלַיִם וְאָמַר לָהֶם
"My children, why do you destroy this city,	בָּנַי מִפְּנֵי מָה אַתֶּם מַחֲרִיבִין אֶת הָעִיר הַזֹּאת
"and why do you seek to burn the Temple?	וְאַתֶּם מְבַקְשִׁים לִשְׂרוֹף אֶת בֵּית הַמִּקְדָּשׁ
"For what is it that he asks of you?	כִּי מַהוּ מְבַקֵּשׁ מִכֶּם
"He asks of you only one bow or one arrow,	אֵינוּ מְבַקֵּשׁ מִכֶּם אֶלָּא קֶשֶׁת אַחַת אוֹ חֵץ אַחַת

56

"and he will go off from you."
They said to him,
"Even as we went forth against
the two before him and slew them,
"so shall we go forth against
him and slay him."

Vespasian had men stationed
near the walls of Jerusalem.
Every word which they
overheard
they would write down,
attach [the message] to an arrow,
and shoot it over the wall,
saying that
Rabban Yohanan ben Zakkai
was one of the Emperor's
supporters.
Now, after Rabban Yohanan
ben Zakkai had spoken to
them one day, two days and
three days,
and they still would not listen
to him,
he sent for his disciples,
for Rabbi Eliezer and Rabbi
Joshua.
"My sons,"
he said to them,
"arise and take me out of here.
"Make a coffin for me that I
might lie in it."
Rabbi Eliezer took the head
end of it,
Rabbi Joshua took hold of the
foot;
and they began carrying him

וַיֵּלֶךְ לוֹ מִכֶּם
אָמְרוּ לוֹ
כְּשֵׁם שֶׁיָּצָאנוּ עַל שְׁנַיִם
שֶׁלְּפָנָיו וַהֲרַגְנוּם
כָּךְ נֵצֵא עָלָיו וְנַהַרְגֵהוּ
הָיוּ לְאַסְפַּסְיָנוּס אֲנָשִׁים
שְׁרוּיִין כְּנֶגֶד חוֹמוֹתֶיהָ שֶׁל
יְרוּשָׁלַיִם

כָּל דָּבָר וְדָבָר שֶׁהָיוּ שׁוֹמְעִין

הָיוּ כּוֹתְבִין
עַל הַחֵצִי
וְזוֹרְקִין חוּץ לַחוֹמָה
לוֹמַר שֶׁרַבָּן
יוֹחָנָן בֶּן זַכַּאי מֵאוֹהֲבֵי
קֵיסָר הוּא

וְכֵיוָן שֶׁאָמַר לָהֶם רַבָּן יוֹחָנָן
בֶּן זַכַּאי
יוֹם אֶחָד וּשְׁנַיִם וּשְׁלֹשָׁה

וְלֹא קִבְּלוּ מִמֶּנּוּ

שָׁלַח לְתַלְמִידָיו
לְרַבִּי אֱלִיעֶזֶר וְרַבִּי יְהוֹשֻׁעַ

בָּנַי
אָמַר לָהֶם
עִמְדוּ וְהוֹצִיאוּנִי מִכָּאן
עֲשׂוּ לִי אָרוֹן וְאִישַׁן בְּתוֹכוֹ

רַבִּי אֱלִיעֶזֶר אָחַז בְּרֹאשׁוֹ

רַבִּי יְהוֹשֻׁעַ אָחַז בְּרַגְלָיו

וְהָיוּ מוֹלִיכִין אוֹתוֹ עַד

57

as the sun set,
until they reached the gates of
    Jerusalem.
"Who is this?"
the gatekeepers demanded.
"It's a dead man," they replied.
"Do you not know that the
    dead may not be held
    overnight in Jerusalem?"
"If it's a dead man," the
    gatekeepers said to them,
    "take him out."
They continued carrying him
until they reached Vespasian.
They opened the coffin,
and [Rabban Yohanan ben
    Zakkai] stood up before him.
[Vespasian] inquired;
"Are you Rabban Yohanan
    ben Zakkai?"
"Tell me, what may I give
    you?"
"I ask of you only Yavneh,
    where I might go
"and teach my disciples
"and there establish a prayer
    [house]

שְׁקִיעַת הַחַמָּה
עַד שֶׁהִגִּיעוּ אֵצֶל שַׁעֲרֵי
יְרוּשָׁלַיִם.
אָמְרוּ לָהֶם הַשּׁוֹעֲרִים
מִי הוּא זֶה
אָמְרוּ לָהֶן מֵת הוּא
אֵין אַתֶּם יוֹדְעִין שֶׁאֵין
מְלִינִים אֶת הַמֵּת בִּירוּשָׁלַיִם

אָמְרוּ לָהֶן אִם מֵת הוּא
הוֹצִיאוּהוּ.

הָיוּ מוֹלִיכִין אוֹתוֹ
עַד שֶׁהִגִּיעוּ אֵצֶל אַסְפַּסְיָינוּס.
פָּתְחוּ הָאָרוֹן
וְעָמַד לְפָנָיו.

אָמַר לוֹ
אַתָּה הוּא רַבָּן יוֹחָנָן בֶּן זַכַּאי

שָׁאַל מָה אֶתֵּן לָךְ

אֵינִי מְבַקֵּשׁ מִמְּךָ אֶלָּא יַבְנֶה
שֶׁאֵלֵךְ
וְאֶשְׁנֶה בָּהּ לְתַלְמִידַי
וְאֶקְבַּע בָּהּ תְּפִלָּה

58

"and perform all the
commandments."
"Go," Vespasian said to him,
"and whatever you wish to do,
do."
Said [Rabban Yohanan] to
him,
"By your leave, may I say
something to you?"
"Speak," [Vespasian] said to
him.
Said [Rabban Yohanan] to
him,
"Lo, you [already] stand as
royalty."
"How do you know this?"
[Vespasian asked].
[Rabban Yohanan] replied,
"This has been handed down
to us,
"that the Temple will not be
surrendered to a commoner,
"but to a king;
"as it is said,
"And he shall cut down the
thickets of the forest with
iron, and Lebanon shall fall
by a mighty one" (Is. 10:34).
It was said:
No more than a day, or two or
three days, passed
before a pair of men reached
him from his city
[announcing]
that the emperor was dead
and that he had been elected
to succeed as king.

וְאֶעֱשֶׂה בָה כָּל מִצְוֹת

אָמַר לוֹ לֵךְ
וְכָל מַה שֶׁאַתָּה רוֹצֶה
לַעֲשׂוֹת עֲשֵׂה.
אָמַר לוֹ

רְצוֹנְךָ שֶׁאוֹמַר לְפָנֶיךָ דָּבָר
אֶחָד
אָמַר לוֹ אֱמוֹר

אָמַר לוֹ

הֲרֵי אַת עוֹמֵד בְּמַלְכוּת

מִנַּיִן אַתָּה יוֹדֵעַ.

אָמַר לוֹ
כָּךְ מָסוּר לָנוּ.

שֶׁאֵין בֵּית הַמִּקְדָּשׁ נִמְסָר
בְּיַד הֶדְיוֹט
אֶלָּא בְּיַד מֶלֶךְ
שֶׁנֶּאֱמַר
וְנִקַּף סִבְכֵי הַיַּעַר בַּבַּרְזֶל
וְהַלְּבָנוֹן בְּאַדִּיר יִפּוֹל

אָמְרוּ
לֹא הָיָה יוֹם אֶחָד שְׁנַיִם
וּשְׁלֹשָׁה יָמִים
עַד שֶׁבָּא אֵלָיו דִּיּוּפְלָא מֵעִירוֹ

שֶׁמֵּת קֵיסַר
וְנִמְנוּ עָלָיו לַעֲמוֹד בְּמַלְכוּת.

Vocabulary

when	כְּשֶׁ...	he took	אָחַז
to destroy	לְהַחֲרִיב	they carry	מוֹלִיכִין
fools	שׁוֹטִים	the sun set	שְׁקִיעַת הַחַמָּה
why	מִפְּנֵי מָה	they reached	הִגִּיעוּ
[you] seek	מְבַקְּשִׁים	who is this	מִי הוּא זֶה
for	לִשְׂרוֹף	gatekeepers	שׁוֹעֲרִים
to burn	כִּי	dead man	מֵת
but	אֶלָּא	[they] hold overnight	מְלִינִים
[you] send!	תְּשַׁגְּרוּ		
bow	קֶשֶׁת	take him out	הוֹצִיאוּהוּ
arrow	חֵץ	they opened	פָּתְחוּ
I shall go	אֵלֵךְ	I shall give	אֶתֵּן
even as	כְּשֵׁם	I only ask	אֵינִי מְבַקֵּשׁ ...
[we] slew them	הֲרַגְנוּם		אֶלָּא
[we shall] go forth	נֵצֵא	I might go	אֵלֵךְ
he sent for	שָׁלַח	I might teach	אֶשְׁנֶה
my children	בָּנַי	my students	תַּלְמִידַי
stationed	שְׁרוּיִין	I will establish	אַקְבַּע
near	כְּנֶגֶד	I will perform	אֶעֱשֶׂה
its walls	הוֹמוֹתֶיהָ	go	לֵךְ
every word	כָּל דָּבָר וְדָבָר	by your leave	רְצוֹנֶךָ
shoot	זוֹרְקִין	you stand as royalty	הֲרֵי אַתְּ עוֹמֵד בְּמַלְכוּת
over	חוּץ	how [whence]	מִנַּיִן
one of	מֵ...	it has been handed down	מָסוּר
friend/supporter	אוֹהֵב	surrendered	נִמְסָר
Emperor	קֵיסָר	commoner	הֶדְיוֹט
they listened	קִבְּלוּ	a pair of men	דְּיוּפְלָא
arise!	עִמְדוּ	his city	עִירוֹ
take me out	הוֹצִיאוּנִי	elected	נִמְנוּ
coffin	אָרוֹן		
I will lie	אִישַׁן		

12. How the Story Works

The story is long. But each part of it is needed so that the story can say all the things it wants to say. In fact, it is like a play in five separate acts, two before the climax, which are matched against one another, then two after the climax, also matched against one another. And there is one in the middle—the climax of the whole story.

What do we mean by "acts" or "parts of the story?" What we mean is that there are a number of little scenes. Each is complete in itself. But one flows right on to the next. These "scenes" in fact are conversations. At each point at which someone new begins to say something, we may count a scene.

So who are the people to talk here?

(Scene One) Vespasian talks to the inhabitants of Jerusalem. He tells them he simply wants them to submit. He will leave them alone. They tell him that they have done it before, and they can do it again.

(Scene Two) Yohanan ben Zakkai talks to the same people. Now he says to them, in the very same words, precisely what Vespasian said. He does make one important change. This shift is so important that the repetition of the same words as Vespasian said is absolutely essential to underline the differences. Vespasian called the people *fools*. Yohanan calls them *My children*. What a difference! But the storyteller has precisely the same ending for both conversations. The people say the same words to Yohanan that they said to Vespasian. They see no difference between sage and general, life and death.

The storyteller admires the sage and is probably a sage himself. He must be shocked by the fact that the people treat the sage exactly as they treat the Roman general. Even though the general called them *fools* and Yohanan called them *children* —and the same word can mean, "disciples"—the people do not see any difference at all. They are just not listening.

This scene ends with a transition, a bridge between what has just happened and what is going to happen.

Vespasian has "men inside the walls." We would call them spies. They write down on a piece of paper and shoot over the wall whatever they think Vespasian would want to hear. Now surely the general is interested to learn that, in the besieged city, one of the great sages takes the view that the people should make peace and go about their business.

(Scene Three) The next conversation is the climax of the story and makes its main point. People talk to one another in a dialogue. This is just like a television story that unfolds not through what you see, but through what people tell you by talking with one another. But the main point now is not the conversation but the scene.

The scene is striking. Yohanan ben Zakkai wants to get out of Jerusalem. So all he needs to do is walk out. But that will not do. The storyteller assumes you know something he has not told you, which is that you cannot walk out of the city. You can only get out if you are dead. The reason—again, we are not told—is that the people in control will not let anyone out.

Why not?

Because they are afraid that if they let people out, many will give up the cause and run away. So they forced the people to stay and fight. That is the kind of leaders they were.

The result is that you could get out of Jerusalem, in the time of siege, only if you were dead. A corpse could not be kept there overnight. So a corpse would be allowed to leave—that is people could take a dead person out of the city.

Since we already know that, so far as they are concerned, Yohanan ben Zakkai, the great sage, is no different from Vespasian, the Roman general, we are prepared for this fact.

Yohanan is going to pretend to have died.

Yohanan lies down in the coffin. His students, Eliezer, whom we already know, and Joshua, whom we shall meet in the next chapter, carry out the coffin.

The gatekeepers ask who is leaving, and they are told it is a corpse. They are treated like ignorant people, "Do you not know . . . ." Once they are told the facts, they let the coffin go through.

Now Yohanan ben Zakkai is brought to the Roman camp, right up to Vespasian's tent. Why the Roman soldiers would let the Jewish sages carry a coffin through their camp, and what they thought was happening, we are not told. You already know that the storyteller will tell you only what you must know, so that he can make his points through what he says—and through what he does not say.

And here is the simple climax: *Yohanan rises from the coffin.*

The coffin is for the dead. Yohanan has gone down into death. And he has risen again—as if from the dead.

He has left the dying city, the city that soon will be dead and full of corpses.

He has come to the heart of the enemy's camp. There, in the face of the cause of death, he rises from the dead.

It is a stunning set of contrasts, so stunning that you can probably make a long list of them.

Then we have two further conversations.

(Scene Four) Yohanan and Vespasian talk: In fact, they have two conversations. In the first one, Vespasian speaks first and controls the conversation. In the second, Yohanan speaks first and runs things.

In the first conversation, Vespasian recognizes Yohanan without being told. He immediately knows it is Yohanan, which is why he asks *whether* it is Yohanan. If he did not know it was Yohanan, he would not have known to ask.

Then he wants to do something for Yohanan because Yohanan is known as a friend of Vespasian.

Yohanan asks for three little things. He wants to go down to a coastal town named Yavneh, which is no longer a battlefield.

There he will (1) teach Torah to his disciples.

And he also will (2) establish a prayer house.

And, finally, he will (3) do all the commandments.

In fact, these three things sum up all of Judaism as the sages shape it. Judaism is a religion that involves (1) study of Torah, (2) saying of prayers, and (3) doing all of the commandments.

So these "three little requests" to Vespasian are hardly so small as they seem.

But to Vespasian they will not appear great. For he is engaged in a great war in the Land of Israel and a great adventure in Rome, as well. He wants to become emperor. He will be an important person.

What is important about the books people choose to read or mumble? Why should Vespasian care whether this old man says his prayers? What difference does it make to him if he teaches his students.

Vespasian knows about philosophers and holy men, with their circles of students or their bands of followers. He knows that these are not the sort of people who can make trouble for Rome or for him.

It is easy enough for him to do a little favor for Yohanan.

(Scene Five) And then at the end, Yohanan will reciprocate and do a favor for Vespasian. It is also—in Yohanan's eyes—just as slight a favor for the Roman general as the right to go to Yavneh was in Vespasian's view.

The thing that matters most to Yohanan is to go to Yavneh and there to teach his students and establish his prayer house and do the commandments.

The thing that matters most to Vespasian is to become emperor.

So Yohanan tells Vespasian that in a short time he will be made king. And the reason he will be made king, even though Vespasian does not know it, is Vespasian's position, here and now, before Jerusalem.

Yohanan believes Vespasian is going to take Jerusalem. He, therefore, knows that soon Vespasian will be emperor.

How does he know it?

Because Yohanan is a master of the Torah. And in the Torah is a verse that says that "Lebanon" will fall by "a mighty one." Now in Yohanan's mind, "Lebanon" refers to the Temple. Perhaps this is because it was built out of cedars cut down in Lebanon and brought to Jerusalem in Solomon's time.

Lebanon will fall to a mighty one—that is to say, in Yohanan's deep understanding of what Isaiah had said a long time ago, to an emperor or a king.

So because of Yohanan's mastery of the Torah, he is able to tell Vespasian what is about to happen in faraway Rome. The end of this part of the story is predictable. What Yohanan said would happen, did happen.

Now let us stand back and go over the five scenes of the play:

(One) Vespasian and the men of Jerusalem

(Two) Yohanan ben Zakkai and the men of Jerusalem

(Three) Yohanan lies down in a coffin and rises up from the coffin.

(Four) Vespasian does a favor for Yohanan, and gives him what he wants most of all.

(Five) Yohanan ben Zakkai does a favor for Vespasian, and gives him what he wants most of all.

So that is the story—a powerful and beautifully constructed drama.

It would not be possible to tell the story more simply, or to say more things in the telling of it. The contrasts—which we have come to expect— are stunning. The points are made not by what the storyteller says to us directly, but by what he puts in the mouths of his characters.

More than this, what the people say in the story is so carefully worded that in the very shift of one single word, "Fools" to "My children," comes the whole message of the sage and the emperor, on the one side, and the sage and the Torah on the other.

The sage calls the people, "My children," because, even though he disagrees with them, he loves them. He cares for them. His message is important because it expresses his concern.

The emperor calls the people, "Fools," because, even though he is their ruler, he does not think much of them. He does not care for them. He only wants them to submit to his rule. His message is unimportant because it does not come out of love.

There is much, much more to be seen in this story. But these are the main points. Now you know why this story is the very soul of the meaning of the destruction of the Second Temple. It tells us who we are. The story explains how Judaism became the religion of Torah and of sages rather than the religion of Temple and of priests.

1. How can you tell when one scene is over and another scene begins?
2. Why do you think the storyteller has laid matters out in two pairs of matched conversations with the action-scene— Yohanan and the coffin—in the middle?
3. What are some of the details the storyteller has not told us? Why do you think he has left them out?
4. Why does Yohanan ben Zakkai agree with Vespasian about what is going to happen? Why do the people of the city disagree with Yohanan?
5. Do you think Yohanan ben Zakkai was a traitor to Jerusalem and its people because he went over to the side of Vespasian? What choices do you think he had?
6. Why did the gatekeepers let the coffin go out? Do you think they should have stabbed the corpse to be sure it was dead? Why does the storyteller not have them stab the corpse?
7. What is the meaning of the three things Yohanan ben Zakkai asks? Do you think Vespasian cared what Yohanan would do in Yavneh? Why does the storyteller place these three things into the center of his story?
8. Why is it important for Yohanan ben Zakkai to tell Vespasian he will be emperor? Do you think the storyteller wants to underline that Vespasian succeeded because the Torah said he should?
9. What do you think the master and disciples would do when they got to Yavneh?
10. If the story is told in five parts, is it easy to memorize five main ideas? Why is it easy to remember five things? Could it be because you have five fingers on your hand? Do you think the fact that the third part is the most important has anything to do with memorizing the parts of the story, one by one?

13. The Power of the Sage

he story of Yohanan ben Zakkai and Vespasian is very long. But it is one continuous story. If you leave out a single detail, the whole thing makes no sense. Let us now see the story as a whole, so that we can discuss it as a whole.

ABOT D'RABBI NATHAN CHAPTER FOUR

כְּשֶׁבָּא אַסְפַּסְיָנוּס לְהַחֲרִיב אֶת יְרוּשָׁלַיִם, אָמַר לָהֶם: שׁוֹטִים, מִפְּנֵי מָה אַתֶּם מְבַקְשִׁים לְהַחֲרִיב אֶת הָעִיר הַזֹּאת וְאַתֶּם מְבַקְשִׁים לִשְׂרוֹף אֶת בֵּית הַמִּקְדָּשׁ? וְכִי מָה אֲנִי מְבַקֵּשׁ מִכֶּם— אֶלָּא שֶׁתְּשַׁגְּרוּ לִי קֶשֶׁת אַחַת אוֹ חֵץ אַחַת, וְאֵלֵךְ לִי מִכֶּם. אָמְרוּ לוֹ: כְּשֵׁם שֶׁיָּצָאנוּ עַל שְׁנַיִם רִאשׁוֹנִים שֶׁהֵם לְפָנֶיךָ וַהֲרַגְנוּם, כָּךְ נֵצֵא לְפָנֶיךָ וְנַהֲרָגֶךָ. כֵּיוָן שֶׁשָּׁמַע רַבָּן יוֹחָנָן בֶּן זַכַּאי, שָׁלַח וְקָרָא לְאַנְשֵׁי יְרוּשָׁלַיִם וְאָמַר לָהֶם: בָּנַי, מִפְּנֵי מָה אַתֶּם מַחֲרִיבִין אֶת הָעִיר הַזֹּאת, וְאַתֶּם מְבַקְשִׁים לִשְׂרוֹף אֶת בֵּית הַמִּקְדָּשׁ? וְכִי מַהוּ מְבַקֵּשׁ מִכֶּם—הָא אֵינוֹ מְבַקֵּשׁ מִכֶּם אֶלָּא קֶשֶׁת אַחַת אוֹ חֵץ אַחַת, וְיֵלֵךְ לוֹ מִכֶּם. אָמְרוּ לוֹ: כְּשֵׁם שֶׁיָּצָאנוּ עַל שְׁנַיִם שֶׁלְּפָנָיו וַהֲרַגְנוּם, כָּךְ נֵצֵא עָלָיו וְנַהֲרְגֵהוּ. הָיוּ לְאַסְפַּסְיָנוּס אֲנָשִׁים שְׁרוּיִין כְּנֶגֶד חוֹמוֹתֶיהָ שֶׁל יְרוּשָׁלַיִם, וְכָל דָּבָר וְדָבָר שֶׁהָיוּ שׁוֹמְעִין הָיוּ כּוֹתְבִין עַל הַחֵצִי, וְזוֹרְקִין חוּץ לַחוֹמָה, לוֹמַר שֶׁרַבָּן יוֹחָנָן בֶּן זַכַּאי מֵאוֹהֲבֵי קֵיסָר הוּא. וְכֵיוָן שֶׁאָמַר לָהֶם רַבָּן יוֹחָנָן בֶּן זַכַּאי יוֹם אֶחָד וּשְׁנַיִם וּשְׁלֹשָׁה וְלֹא קִבְּלוּ מִמֶּנּוּ, שָׁלַח וְקָרָא לְתַלְמִידָיו, לְרַבִּי אֱלִיעֶזֶר וְרַבִּי יְהוֹשֻׁעַ. אָמַר לָהֶם: בָּנַי, עִמְדוּ וְהוֹצִיאוּנִי מִכָּאן. עֲשׂוּ לִי אָרוֹן וְאִישַׁן בְּתוֹכוֹ. רַבִּי אֱלִיעֶזֶר אָחַז בְּרֹאשׁוֹ, רַבִּי יְהוֹשֻׁעַ אָחַז בְּרַגְלָיו, וְהָיוּ מוֹלִיכִין אוֹתוֹ עַד שְׁקִיעַת הַחַמָּה, עַד שֶׁהִגִּיעוּ אֵצֶל שַׁעֲרֵי יְרוּשָׁלַיִם. אָמְרוּ לָהֶם הַשּׁוֹעֲרִים: מִי הוּא זֶה? אָמְרוּ לָהֶן: מֵת הוּא. וְכִי אֵין אַתֶּם יוֹדְעִין שֶׁאֵין מְלִינִין אֶת הַמֵּת בִּירוּשָׁלַיִם? אָמְרוּ לָהֶן: אִם מֵת הוּא, הוֹצִיאוּהוּ. וְהוֹצִיאוּהוּ וְהָיוּ מוֹלִיכִין אוֹתוֹ, עַד שֶׁהִגִּיעוּ אֵצֶל אַסְפַּסְיָנוּס. פָּתְחוּ הָאָרוֹן וְעָמַד לְפָנָיו. אָמַר לוֹ: אַתָּה הוּא רַבָּן יוֹחָנָן בֶּן זַכַּאי? שְׁאַל מָה אֶתֵּן לָךְ? אָמַר לוֹ: אֵינִי מְבַקֵּשׁ מִמְּךָ אֶלָּא יַבְנֶה שֶׁאֵלֵךְ וְאֶשְׁנֶה בָּהּ לְתַלְמִידַי וְאֶקְבַּע בָּהּ תְּפִלָּה, וְאֶעֱשֶׂה בָּהּ כָּל מִצְוֹת. אָמַר לוֹ: לֵךְ, וְכָל מַה שֶּׁאַתָּה רוֹצֶה לַעֲשׂוֹת עֲשֵׂה. אָמַר לוֹ: רְצוֹנְךָ שֶׁאוֹמַר לְפָנֶיךָ דָּבָר אֶחָד? אָמַר לוֹ:

הֲרֵי אַתָּה עוֹמֵד בְּמַלְכוּת. מִנַּיִן אַתָּה יוֹדֵעַ? אָמַר לוֹ: כָּךְ מָסוּר לָנוּ
שֶׁאֵין בֵּית הַמִּקְדָּשׁ נִמְסָר בְּיַד הֶדְיוֹט אֶלָּא בְּיַד מֶלֶךְ, שֶׁנֶּאֱמַר: וְנִקַּף
סִבְכֵי הַיַּעַר בַּבַּרְזֶל וְהַלְּבָנוֹן בְּאַדִּיר יִפּוֹל. אָמְרוּ: לֹא הָיָה יוֹם אֶחָד
שְׁנַיִם וּשְׁלֹשָׁה יָמִים, עַד שֶׁבָּא אֵלָיו דְּיוּפְלָא מֵעִירוֹ שֶׁמֵּת קֵיסָר,
וְנִמְנוּ עָלָיו לַעֲמוֹד בְּמַלְכוּת.

When Vespasian came to destroy Jerusalem he said to the inhabitants, "Fools, why do you seek to destroy this city, and why
do you seek to burn the Temple? For what do I ask of you but
that you send me one bow or one arrow, and I shall leave you?"
They said to him, "Even as we went forth against the first two
who were here before thee and slew them, so shall we go forth
against thee and slay thee." When Rabban Yohanan ben Zakkai
heard this, he sent for the men of Jerusalem and said to them,
"My children, why do you destroy this city, and why do you
seek to burn the Temple? For what is it that he asks of you? He
asks of you only one bow or one arrow, and he will go off from
you." They said to him, "Even as we went forth against the two
before him and slew them, so shall we go forth against him and
slay him." Vespasian had men stationed near the walls of
Jerusalem. Every word which they overheard they would write
down, attach [the message] to an arrow and shoot it over the
wall, saying that Rabban Yohanan ben Zakkai was one of the
Emperor's supporters. Now, after Rabban Yohanan ben Zakkai
had spoken to them one day, two days and three days, and they
still would not listen to him, he sent for his disciples, for Rabbi
Eliezer and Rabbi Joshua. "My sons," he said to them, "arise
and take me out of here. Make a coffin for me that I might lie in
it." Rabbi Eliezer took the head end of it, Rabbi Joshua took
hold of the foot; and they began carrying him as the sun set, until
they reached the gates of Jerusalem. "Who is this?" the
gatekeepers demanded. "It's a dead man," they replied. "Do you
not know that the dead may not be held overnight in
Jerusalem?" "If it's a dead man," the gatekeepers said to them,
"take him out." They continued carrying him until they

reached Vespasian. They opened the coffin, and [Rabban Yohanan ben Zakkai] stood up before him. "Are you Rabban Yohanan ben Zakkai?" [Vespasian] inquired; "Tell me, what may I give you?" "I ask of you only Yavneh, where I might go and teach my disciples and there establish a prayer [house] and perform all the commandments." "Go," Vespasian said to him, "and whatever you wish to do, do." Said [Rabban Yohanan] to him, "By your leave, may I say something to you?" "Speak," [Vespasian] said to him. Said [Rabban Yohanan] to him, "Lo, you [already] stand as royalty." "How do you know this?" [Vespasian asked]. [Rabban Yohanan] replied, "This has been handed down to us, that the Temple will not be surrendered to a commoner, but to a king; as it is said, And he shall cut down the thickets of the forest with iron, and Lebanon shall fall by a mighty one" (Is. 10:34). It was said: No more than a day, or two or three days, passed before a pair of men reached him from his city [announcing] that the emperor was dead and that he had been elected to succeed as king.

o understand the full power of this story, there is one more thing you have to know: the meaning of the place, Yavneh.

"Let me go to Yavneh," is what Yohanan ben Zakkai asked of Vespasian.

We already know that the storyteller takes for granted that we know famous sayings. So when he tells us—without a word of explanation—that Yohanan ben Zakkai wants to go to Yavneh, he knows that we know what happened in Yavneh.

If we do not know what happened in Yavneh, we miss the real point of the story.

In Yavneh, Yohanan ben Zakkai founded a great center for the study of Torah. But the sages of that center also became the government of the Jews of the Land of Israel in the decades after the destruction of the Temple in 70.

In other words, everyone who hears the story learns about Yavneh.

That is the place in which the Jews learned through sages to govern themselves, even while living within the Roman empire, not as an independent nation. The lessons of Yavneh guided the Jews for the next 2,000 years.

The irony of the story is clear. Vespasian thought that he was going to conquer the Jews. But the Jews came out able to rule themselves. Even though they ultimately gave over that bow and arrow, which meant they accepted Roman rule, "our sages" saved them and organized a government for them.

Vespasian thought that he was going to become emperor because he was strong. But Yohanan ben Zakkai told him the truth, which is that he would become emperor only because he had the "merit" of taking Jerusalem and burning the Temple.

And what that meant is simple: Yohanan was saying that the conqueror of the Temple was able to do it because of one thing alone. God had permitted it.

For no one who heard this story imagined that Vespasian could have conquered the Temple if God had *not* wanted him to.

Let us stand back and ask what we have learned about the sage.

First, we must find out how the sage knew so much. How did Yohanan ben Zakkai know that Vespasian was going to destroy Jerusalem and burn the Temple if the people did not submit to him? Was he merely a wise man?

The storyteller's opinion comes at the end, when he has Yohanan cite the verse of Isaiah to Vespasian.

The storyteller does not believe that Yohanan ben Zakkai was merely wise. He believes that Yohanan ben Zakkai knew what was going to happen *because Yohanan knew Scripture.*

That brings up a second matter, which is even more important in this story: the biblical passages of which it reminds us, without citing them at all.

Specifically, if you look in the biblical book of Jeremiah, you will see another example of someone who in a time of siege tells the people to surrender. Jeremiah believes that Nebuchadnezzar, king of the Babylonians, is the rod of God's anger. He is going to take Jerusalem and destroy the Temple because God wants to punish the Jews for their sins.

Jeremiah predicts that Jerusalem will fall to Babylonia.

If you look at the Book of Jeremiah, Chapter Twenty, you see that Jeremiah is at odds with the Jerusalemites of his day. The same is clear in Chapter Twenty-one, Chapter Twenty-two, and elsewhere in the

prophecies of Jeremiah.

Further, when the Babylonians do take Jerusalem, Jeremiah is well treated (Chapter Thirty-nine).

And there is one final point. Jeremiah makes provision for the future. He buys a piece of ground, even when everyone thought that it was all over for the people of Israel in their Land. He did this to make sure people knew that there was hope and a future for the people and Land of Israel.

In the light of these passages in Jeremiah (and many others, which say much the same thing), the story about Yohanan ben Zakkai and his dealings with Vespasian takes on depth. We realize that Yohanan is acting like the prophet Jeremiah. (Later we shall see a miracle-worker who will remind us of Balaam, the gentile prophet.)

Since Yohanan ben Zakkai could read the same chapters of Jeremiah as we can, it is clear that his great wisdom in dealing with the crisis posed by Rome is based on his knowledge of the Torah. In this case it is the book of Jeremiah.

Yohanan ben Zakkai was not a prophet, but he had learned what the prophets said and did. Above all, he was wise enough to make use of his knowledge of Scriptures.

What makes a sage a sage is his power of mind. The power of the sage is his capacity to take seriously the things he learns in Torah. He has the ability to make use of the Torah to make sense of his own times.

So the power of the sage is his knowledge of Torah. That is why people listen to him. That is why even emperors-to-be are wise if they listen to the sage.

This power is strange. It is the strength to face generals and to defy the popular opinion of the day ("fight Rome, do not submit"). Just as everyone was against Vespasian, as their enemy, so everyone probably was against Yohanan, as a traitor.

Yohanan defied everybody and everything, even death. He lay down in a coffin, as if to die. He rose up in the midst of the enemy camp, a place of death for Israel—the Jewish people. And from death he went on to renewed life, to the old-new life of the sage, teaching disciples, studying Torah, doing commandments, saying prayers.

How simple! How safe for Rome! Nothing can come from Yavneh. Only mighty Rome will rule. But that is not how things turned out.

The Jewish people lived on long after the fall of Rome. Thousands of years later, *few people besides* the Jews remember Vespasian. Vespasian thought he won when he destroyed Jerusalem. But the people of Israel survived and endured. Vespasian did destroy Jerusalem, but the Jewish people took the path that led to Yavneh. And that path, in time to come, would lead them back to Jerusalem.

1. What did Yohanan ben Zakkai do at Yavneh that made such a big difference? Why did his program of (1) teaching disciples, (2) praying, and (3) performing the commandments matter so much?

2. Do you think the Jews would have had reason to go forward, had Yohanan ben Zakkai not told them what they might do after the Temple would be no more? What other things might they have done?

3. Why did Vespasian believe he had conquered the Jews? Was he right? Why did Yohanan ben Zakkai take for

granted Vespasian would never conquer the Jews?

4. How did the sage know so much? Why did Scripture tell
   him what he needed to know?

5. Do you think the story of Jeremiah influenced Yohanan
   ben Zakkai? What points do the two stories have in common? What are the differences?

6. Did Yohanan ben Zakkai speak in the name of God? Or in
   the name of Torah? What is the difference?

7. How would you compare the prophet, Jeremiah, with the
   sage, Yohanan ben Zakkai? In what way are they like one
   another? Do you think that not holding any official job
   made any difference? Were they both men of moral authority?

8. In what ways were Jeremiah and Yohanan ben Zakkai not
   like one another? Was it easier for Jeremiah to predict what
   would happen because God told him what to prophesy? Do
   you think Yohanan ben Zakkai would have been wiser had
   he been a prophet, too?

9. Why did both Jeremiah and Yohanan ben Zakkai believe
   that the Jews would have a future in the Land of Israel?
   Why does Jeremiah buy land? Why does Yohanan ben Zakkai ask for the right to go to Yavneh? What importance does
   the Holy Land itself have for both men?

10. Several times we have commented on the power of this
    story. Does the story have the power to stimulate your
    imagination? Can you write a dialogue to take place today
    between Yohanan ben Zakkai and Vespasian? What other
    things would the two men talk about? What do you think
    Yohanan ben Zakkai would tell Vespasian if he could meet
    him today? What Scriptures would he quote to Vespasian?

PART FOUR

How Do Sages Study Torah?

14. How Do Sages Study Torah?

The story about Yohanan ben Zakkai and Vespasian makes the sage into something close to a prophet, a man of God, a person to whom God speaks. But the sage is supposed to be a master of Torah, a man to whom, and through whom, Torah speaks.

And this raises a difficult question. If God revealed the Torah, and the sage knows the Torah, why should God continue to intervene.

Is not the Torah sufficient, so that God may now stand back and let men work things out on their own (in our day: men *and women*).

Let me spell out this issue.

God gave the Torah a long time ago, we believe, and the Torah is there for us to study and to master. So we have to ask whether the people who master the Torah and who become like Moses, our rabbi, are able to communicate, through what they know, with Heaven. Torah comes from Heaven. It is from God. Is there need for more than Torah from God?

Again, if the Torah is God's will and word for Israel, the Jewish people, then do the people who are masters of Torah speak in God's behalf? And if that is the case, can not God join in those discussions and renew prophecy?

But if prophecy—that is, God's speaking to people here on earth—continues, *who needs sages?* Of what purpose is learning? Why should we work hard and learn Torah, if we can get the same truth more readily through God's direct word to prophets and to other holy people?

There is a conflict between the idea that Torah is given to people to learn and the notion that Torah is God's word. For if Torah is God's word, then there can be more words. Torah no longer is all that God wishes to say to us.

To put it differently, how whole and complete is "the one whole Torah of Moses, our rabbi," if there is the possibility that God will add to what already is in the Torah?

For the sages this is an important problem. You realize it because Yohanan ben Zakkai's story shows how the sage is able to predict the future, just like the prophet. That story also shows that the way sages do things is shaped by the way prophets do things.

Now this problem will be spelled out in a dramatic way, as you would expect.

In the time of the sages, as in our own day, people argued with one another about important matters of the Torah. They gave reasons for the positions they took. They gave more reasons to show that the positions of the other side were wrong.

They cited the evidence of the written Torah to prove they were right and the other side was wrong. They might even have cited earlier sages on their side and against the other.

These are not arguments that can be settled. If both sides can cite Torah, then there must be an element of truth in the opinion of each. If both sides can point to great sages in the past whose opinions or whose reasoning seem to support their positions, then both sides have something worth saying.

It follows that the Torah can bring about many sorts of honest and honorable differences of opinion.

How are these to be settled?

The sages take a vote. They hear all the arguments. Then, knowing there is truth on both sides, they still come to a decision. For people had to know not the truth but the law, and how to do what the law required.

But there is another way to appeal to God to give an opinion.

In ancient times, people believed that an unusual event in nature was an omen, a sign, of what Heaven thought.

In the story before us one of the sages calls upon Heaven to intervene. Heaven is to take a position in an argument between two rabbis.

And the strange thing is that, according to the storyteller, Heaven was thinking of doing just that. But that is not how matters come out.

The storyteller raises a deep question and answers it in a deep way. This story, as the one about Yohanan ben Zakkai and Vespasian, reveals who the sages really are.

1. Why would anybody suppose a sage is a holy man?
2. In what way is a sage like a prophet?
3. If the sage is like a prophet, then why should he not claim that God speaks through him now, and not merely through what is written in the Torah?
4. Why is there a contradiction between God speaking through the Torah, which people can learn, and God speaking through the sage directly? Why would people be bothered by that idea? Would it make learning more important or less important?
5. When people speak of "one whole Torah of Moses, our rabbi," do they claim that the Torah is complete? If they do, then what is the possibility that they wish to deny?
6. Why must there be truth on both sides, if each side can cite a verse of Scripture or an opinion of a sage? Can two opposed opinions both be right? Half right? What will be right about each one?
7. Why do you think the rabbis settled arguments by voting? Why would the vote of sages make a difference and so decide the law?
8. Since keeping the law as the Torah teaches it is our duty to Heaven, does the idea that rabbis or sages can vote and decide the law mean that sages also are holy men?
9. Does the idea that sages vote tell us that the sages are democratic? Or does it mean that they have special insight and special power?
10. Do people nowadays believe that events of nature reveal something supernatural? If someone is nearly struck by lightning, does the person believe that the narrow escape means something special? What are the sorts of meanings people might come up with?

15. Torah on Earth and Torah in Heaven

ELIEZER AND JOSHUA DEBATE AN ISSUE OF TORAH, AND HEAVEN IS ASKED TO JOIN THE DISCUSSION
Babylonian Talmud Baba' Mesia' 59a-b

Eliezer and Joshua were students of Yohanan ben Zakkai. They went with him to Yavneh. In later life each one of them became a great sage and had disciples of his own.

In this story, the two men argue about a rather minor matter. What makes the story interesting is that Eliezer does not succeed in persuading people through his excellent arguments.

So he asks Heaven, through nature, to join in the argument. And, the storyteller tells us, Heaven does just that. A carob-tree, a stream of water, and even the walls of the schoolhouse do what Eliezer asks.

Then Joshua intervenes and tells the walls to mind their own business.

The story goes forward. Eliezer calls on Heaven and says that a voice should come forth and tell the truth. So an "echo" is heard. The echo announces that people should not even *argue* with Eliezer because the law accords with his views.

But Joshua has the last word.

He is a sage. Like his teacher—and Eliezer's teacher, Yohanan ben Zakkai—he is able to find in Scripture the necessary guidance.

And Scripture announces plainly that the Torah is not in Heaven. It is not in Heaven because it is given over to the sages. Sages master it, learn how to think in the right way in it, and then make the decisions which, without the Torah, Heaven might join in making.

This is a stunning story. It does not end there, as you will see. It is also a story made up of a number of different contributions. We shall now pay some attention to the diverse hands that have helped to put it all together.

BABYLONIAN TALMUD BABA' MESIA' 59a-b

On that day R. Eliezer brought forward all of the arguments in the world, but they did not accept [them] from him. Said he to them, "If the law agrees with me, "let this carob-tree prove it." The carob-tree was torn a hundred cubits out of its place.

בְּאוֹתוֹ הַיּוֹם הֵשִׁיב רַבִּי אֱלִיעֶזֶר כָּל תְּשׁוּבוֹת שֶׁבָּעוֹלָם וְלֹא קִבְּלוּ הֵימֶנּוּ אָמַר לָהֶם: אִם הֲלָכָה כְּמוֹתִי הֶחָרוּב זֶה יוֹכִיחַ! נֶעֱקַר חָרוּב מִמְּקוֹמוֹ מֵאָה אַמָּה

They said to him, "No proof can be brought from a carob-tree," He said to them, "If the law agrees with me, "let the stream of water prove it." The stream of water flowed backwards.

אָמְרוּ לוֹ אֵין מְבִיאִין רְאָיָה מִן הֶחָרוּב אָמַר לָהֶם אִם הֲלָכָה כְּמוֹתִי אַמַּת הַמַּיִם יוֹכִיחוּ! חָזְרוּ אַמַּת הַמַּיִם לַאֲחוֹרֵיהֶם

They said to him, "No proof can be brought from a stream of water." Again he said to them, "If the law agrees with me, "let the walls of the schoolhouse prove it." The walls inclined to fall. R. Joshua rebuked them, saying, "When disciples of sages are engaged in a legal dispute, "what is your value?"

אָמְרוּ לוֹ: אֵין מְבִיאִין רְאָיָה מֵאַמַּת הַמַּיִם חָזַר וְאָמַר לָהֶם: אִם הֲלָכָה כְּמוֹתִי כָּתְלֵי בֵּית הַמִּדְרָשׁ יוֹכִיחוּ! הִטּוּ כָּתְלֵי בֵּית הַמִּדְרָשׁ לִפֹּל גָּעַר בָּהֶם רַבִּי יְהוֹשֻׁעַ, אָמַר לָהֶם: אִם תַּלְמִידֵי חֲכָמִים מְנַצְּחִים זֶה אֶת זֶה בַּהֲלָכָה — אַתֶּם מַה טִּיבְכֶם!

Hence they did not fall,

לֹא נָפְלוּ

81

in honor of R. Joshua,
nor did they resume the
   upright,
in honor of R. Eliezer,
[And they still are standing
   thus inclined.]
Again he said to them,
"If the law agrees with me,
"let it be proved from
   Heaven."
An echo went forth and said,
"Why do you dispute with R.
   Eliezer,
"for in all matters the law
   agrees with him!"
But R. Joshua arose and
   exclaimed,
"*It is not in heaven* (Deut.
   30:12)."
R. Nathan met Elijah
and asked him,
"What did the Holy One,
   blessed be He, do at that
   time?"
He replied,
"He laughed [with joy],
"saying, 'My sons have
   defeated Me.
" 'My sons have defeated
   me.' "

מִפְּנֵי כְבוֹדוֹ שֶׁל רַבִּי יְהוֹשֻׁעַ
וְלֹא זָקְפוּ

מִפְּנֵי כְבוֹדוֹ שֶׁל רַבִּי אֱלִיעֶזֶר
וַעֲדַיִן מַטִּין וְעוֹמְדִין

חָזַר וְאָמַר לָהֶם:
אִם הֲלָכָה כְּמוֹתִי
מִן הַשָּׁמַיִם יוֹכִיחוּ!

יָצְאתָה בַּת קוֹל וְאָמְרָה:
מַה לָכֶם אֵצֶל רַבִּי אֱלִיעֶזֶר

שֶׁהֲלָכָה כְּמוֹתוֹ בְּכָל מָקוֹם.

עָמַד רַבִּי יְהוֹשֻׁעַ עַל רַגְלָיו
וְאָמַר:
לֹא בַשָּׁמַיִם הוּא

אַשְׁכְּחֵיהּ רַבִּי נָתָן לְאֵלִיָּהוּ
אָמַר לֵיהּ:
מַאי עָבֵד קֻדְשָׁא בְּרִיךְ הוּא
בְּהַהִיא שַׁעֲתָא?

אָמַר לֵיהּ
קָא חָיֵךְ
וְאָמַר: נִצְּחוּנִי בָּנַי

נִצְּחוּנִי בָּנַי

82

Vocabulary

brought forward	הֵשִׁיב	rebuked	גָּעַר
arguments	תְּשׁוּבוֹת	disciples of	תַּלְמִידֵי חֲכָמִים
world	עוֹלָם	the sages	
accept	קִבְּלוּ	engage in	מְנַצְּחִים בַּהֲלָכָה
from him	הֵימֶנּוּ	legal dispute	
law	הֲלָכָה	your value	טִיבְכֶם
with me	כְּמוֹתִי	because of	מִפְּנֵי
carob-tree	חָרוּב	honor	כָּבוֹד
prove	יוֹכִיחַ	resume the upright	זָקְפוּ
torn	נֶעֱקַר	still	עֲדַיִן
place	מָקוֹם	went forth	יָצְאָתָה
cubit	אַמָּה	echo	בַּת קוֹל
bring	מְבִיאִין	in all matters	בְּכָל מָקוֹם
proof	רְאָיָה	meet	אַשְׁכַּח
stream	אַמַּת	what	מַאי
backwards	לַאֲחוֹרֵיהֶם	do	עֲבַד
said again	חָזַר וְאָמַר	the Holy One,	קֻדְשָׁא בְּרִיךְ
wall	כֹּתֶל	blessed be He	הוּא
schoolhouse	בֵּית הַמִּדְרָשׁ	time	שָׁעֲתָא
inclined	הִטּוּ	laughed	חַיֵּךְ
to fall	לִפֹּל	defeated me	נִצְּחוּנִי

16.
How the
Story Works

This is a dramatic story. It makes an important point about sages. It gives the sages the power to set aside supernatural or miraculous signs and wonders.

The point of the story is Joshua's. The learning of the sages is so powerful that it overcomes what Heaven says. That is to say, when we seek the truth, we look for it through argument, reason and logic. We make use of our own minds.

We do not rely on trees, rivers, or even man-made walls to tell us what is true.

The story makes its point twice. First, there is a matched set of three exchanges.

Then there is the second, and separate, conversation between Joshua and the heavenly echo—a voice from Heaven.

At the end there is the wonderful conversation between Nathan and the prophet Elijah.

Let us go over each of the parts of the story and then see how they work together to create a single picture.

The first unit has three entries, each in precisely the same form and pattern:

(1) Let the tree prove my case, and the tree does it.

(2) Let the stream prove my case, and the stream proves it.

(3) Let the very walls of the schoolhouse prove it, and the walls begin to fall but stop when Joshua tells them off.

Clearly, the story reaches its climax at the third element in the triplet, when the pattern shifts.

The first two parts say the same thing. It is only when Joshua tells the walls not to interfere in the discussions of the sages within the walls that the main point comes through. So the walls are made to testify by being neutral and not taking the side of one or the other of the two sages.

This way of story-telling, by giving three incidents, is familiar to you. It is commonplace. If you only had the first unit, you would see no pattern. The second entry is necessary to establish the pattern. And then the third entry comes to power by breaking that same pattern.

The same point is made again. This time, the whole situation is clearer. Now, however, in addition to the trees, rivers and buildings, Heaven joins in. People believed that an "echo" carried supernatural messages in the same way "the word of the Lord" did during the times of the prophets. So the echo is a strong testimony.

Eliezer calls on Heaven to prove his point. The "echo" says Eliezer is right—not only now, but under *all* circumstances!

Here comes Joshua's powerful reply.

He is a master of Torah, a sage. Torah stands against Heaven—which gave Torah.

So Joshua does something stunning: he quotes Heaven against Heaven. His learning in Torah is such that he can cite the word of Torah against this later word of Torah.

The main point of this story is that when sages and Heaven disagree, sages win out. Heaven stands back. Why? Because God wants the sages to use their minds. Their learning in Torah is more powerful than miracles and wonders. God wants sages to be independent in mind because their minds are learned in Torah.

The message of the "echo" is inconsistent with the word of Torah. So the "echo" must be wrong. Joshua evokes Heaven to rebuke Heaven's message: Torah takes precedence over whatever would be sent forth later on.

Joshua quotes a verse from Moses telling the children of Israel not to say that the Torah is far off. The Torah is in the midst of the people, not in Heaven.

The sage understands Moses to say, "You don't need prophets or miracle-workers to go up to Heaven and get Torah. Torah is in your midst. The sage, who is the man of Torah and the master of Torah, gives Torah here and now. *So it is not in heaven.*"

These two stories create an unbearable conflict between the Torah and the Lord. After all, Heaven has said that the law follows Eliezer. But Joshua tells Heaven to keep quiet. Is not Heaven (that is to say, the Lord) going to be displeased?

After all, suppose you have a fight with your brother or sister, and your father or mother comes along to intervene. Then you tell your parent, "Keep out of it because you promised to keep out of it"—will your father or mother be happy about it?

Even though your parent will do what you say, there will be some

unhappiness.

That is the tension created by the two stories. It is one thing to rebuke nature. It is quite another to tell Heaven to be silent and go away.

And that is what Joshua has done.

So the third and final element of the story—Nathan's report of Elijah's account of the events that day in Heaven—is absolutely necessary. It answers a question that the two previous stories raise. And it does so in a stunning way. Now we see that it comes as the climax of the whole construction, and therefore, as its conclusion.

Elijah says that God sees the sages as children, as "his sons," and just as a parent is happy when his or her sons do well, so God is happy that the sons have thought of the only possible, and right, answer. By losing to the sons, that is the sages, God is overjoyed.

Why?

Sages follow the model of Moses, our rabbi, who is in the image of God. It follows, therefore, that God rejoices in the sages, who are in his image.

We see that the three stories—the natural wonders, the echo from Heaven, and the Elijah-story—form a complete and unified story.

The first sets the stage for the second, by dismissing the power of nature.

The second sets the stage for the third, by creating an unbearable tension.

And the third resolves the problem of the whole.

Torah places limits even upon Heaven, perhaps *especially* upon Heaven.

We see, once more, how carefully the stories before us are put together. They are constructed to make a particular point. The storyteller does not have to say it in so many words; he sets it forth in a few brief sentences.

But he follows a pattern by using groups of threes or fives. The pattern may be subdivided, as it is in the first unit of this construction. At the high point of the pattern—the third item of three, the third item of five (in the story of Vespasian and Yohanan ben Zakkai)—the wise storyteller will make his point. He does not have to repeat it because he has made it obvious. It is more than obvious, it is stunning.

The main point will resolve all the tensions created by the preceding elements. You will have no doubt whatsoever of the truth the storyteller wants you to know.

When you study Mishnah and Talmud in these books, you will see that matters are put together with the same thought and care. The words are so carefully chosen that they add up to little poems.

1. Why do you think the storyteller uses three examples to tell his first story?
2. Do you think you can learn something from the way the storyteller tells the story, as well as from what he says in his story?
3. Is there a difference between the tree and the stream, as there is a difference—natural *vs.* man-made objects—between the stream or the trees and the walls of the schoolhouse?
4. Why does Joshua not have to quote a line of Torah when he answers the tree, the stream, and the walls of the schoolhouse? Would it have been a false note if he had at that point found an appropriate verse of Scripture?
5. Why would people have believed the "echo" from Heaven?

Do you think that Joshua did not believe the "echo" at all, or did he have a different viewpoint from the "echo"?

6. What is the meaning of the verse that Joshua quotes? If you look up the verse you will find that the entire passage is appropriate for Joshua's case. Is there any difference between the meaning of the passage and the way in which Joshua uses the passage in the setting of his argument? Or do both Deuteronomy and the storyteller have the same idea in mind?

7. What is the meaning of Joshua's citing a verse of the Torah against the testimony of Heaven? Why is this a powerful rebuke? Does Joshua accuse Heaven of mind-changing and inconsistency?

8. What is the difference between a sage and a miracle-worker? Does the storyteller, who is a sage, think that sages need to make miracles in order to be believed?

9. What do you think a sage would say to a miracle-worker? Do sages believe in miracles? Do they do miracles? If they do believe, then why do they not do miracles? Does Torah represent another kind of power in the world?

10. Why is God happy that Joshua has cited the right verse and answered God back in that way? Why does God call the sages "my sons"? Does the word for "son" mean something else? Did you notice that Yohanan ben Zakkai used the same word for the inhabitants of Jerusalem, and also for Eliezer? Do you think the word means "my students" and "my disciples"? Or does it mean, "my children" in a more general sense? Are women excluded then? Are they excluded today?

17. The Power of Torah

W e now realize that the "three stories" form one. The story, as a whole, creates a conflict and then resolves it. The conflict is between Torah and Heaven, between the sage and the supernatural. The resolution comes when the Torah and the sage are shown to be more powerful than Heaven and the supernatural.

But the power of the sage comes from Torah, which is the work of Heaven. So the real point is that Torah and nature are creations of God, and nature cannot take precedence over Torah. Nor is the supernatural more powerful than Torah—for the very same reason. God is limited by the Torah, as much as nature is limited by the Torah. To see how all this is said, let us now reread the story as a whole.

BABYLONIAN TALMUD BABA' MESIA' 59b

בְּאוֹתוֹ הַיּוֹם הֵשִׁיב רַבִּי אֱלִיעֶזֶר כָּל תְּשׁוּבוֹת שֶׁבָּעוֹלָם
וְלֹא קִבְּלוּ הֵימֶנּוּ. אָמַר לָהֶם: אִם הֲלָכָה כְּמוֹתִי—חָרוּב זֶה יוֹכִיחַ!
נֶעֱקַר חָרוּב מִמְּקוֹמוֹ מֵאָה אַמָּה; אָמְרוּ לוֹ: אֵין מְבִיאִין רְאָיָה מִן
הֶחָרוּב. חָזַר וְאָמַר לָהֶם: אִם הֲלָכָה כְּמוֹתִי—אַמַּת הַמַּיִם יוֹכִיחוּ!
חָזְרוּ אַמַּת הַמַּיִם לַאֲחוֹרֵיהֶם; אָמְרוּ לוֹ: אֵין מְבִיאִין רְאָיָה מֵאַמַּת
הַמָּיִם. חָזַר וְאָמַר לָהֶם: אִם הֲלָכָה כְּמוֹתִי—כָּתְלֵי בֵּית הַמִּדְרָשׁ
יוֹכִיחוּ! הִטּוּ כָּתְלֵי בֵּית הַמִּדְרָשׁ לִפֹּל; גָּעַר בָּהֶם רַבִּי יְהוֹשֻׁעַ, אָמַר
לָהֶם: אִם תַּלְמִידֵי חֲכָמִים מְנַצְּחִים זֶה אֶת זֶה בַּהֲלָכָה—אַתֶּם מַה
טִּיבְכֶם! לֹא נָפְלוּ מִפְּנֵי כְּבוֹדוֹ שֶׁל רַבִּי יְהוֹשֻׁעַ, וְלֹא זָקְפוּ מִפְּנֵי
כְּבוֹדוֹ שֶׁל רַבִּי אֱלִיעֶזֶר, וַעֲדַיִן מַטִּין וְעוֹמְדִין. חָזַר וְאָמַר לָהֶם: אִם
הֲלָכָה כְּמוֹתִי—מִן הַשָּׁמַיִם יוֹכִיחוּ! יָצְאתָה בַּת קוֹל וְאָמְרָה:
מַה לָכֶם אֵצֶל רַבִּי אֱלִיעֶזֶר, שֶׁהֲלָכָה כְּמוֹתוֹ בְּכָל מָקוֹם. עָמַד רַבִּי
יְהוֹשֻׁעַ עַל רַגְלָיו וְאָמַר: לֹא בַשָּׁמַיִם הִוא! אַשְׁכְּחֵיהּ רַבִּי נָתָן
לְאֵלִיָּהוּ, אָמַר לֵיהּ: מַאי עָבֵד קֻדְשָׁא בְּרִיךְ הוּא בְּהַהִיא שַׁעֲתָא?
אָמַר לֵיהּ, קָא חָיֵךְ וְאָמַר: נִצְּחוּנִי בָנַי, נִצְּחוּנִי בָּנַי.

On that day R. Eliezer brought forward all of the arguments in the world, but they did not accept [them] from him. Said he to them, "If the law agrees with me, let this carob-tree prove it." The carob-tree was torn a hundred cubits out of its place. They said to him, "No proof can be brought from a carob-tree." He said to them, "If the law agrees with me, let the stream of water prove it." The stream of water flowed backwards. They said to him, "No proof can be brought from a stream of water." Again he said to them, "If the law agrees with me, let the walls of the schoolhouse prove it." The walls inclined to fall. R. Joshua rebuked them, saying, "When disciples of sages are engaged in a legal dispute, what is your value?" Hence they did not fall, in honor of R. Joshua, nor did they resume the upright, in honor of R. Eliezer. [And they still are standing thus inclined.] Again he said to them, "If the law agrees with me, let it be proved from Heaven." An echo went forth and said, "Why do you dispute with R. Eliezer, for in all matters the law agrees with him!" But R. Joshua arose and exclaimed, "*It is not in heaven* (Deut. 30:12)." R. Nathan met Elijah and asked him, "What did the Holy One, blessed be He, do at that time?" He replied, "He laughed [with joy], saying, 'My sons have defeated Me. My sons have defeated me.' "

he one thing that the storyteller does not tell us is the subject of the argument. You might suppose that it is on some weighty matter of religious teaching. But it is not. At issue is a certain kind of oven. The question is the status of that oven under a certain special circumstance. In other words, the deepest irony of the story is the fact that the issue is something so small and picayune. It is as if you had a big fight in your synagogue about whether the president of the synagogue sits on the left hand or on the right hand of the rabbi. True, it is an issue. But for such an issue, you do not go to war.

So the claim of the story is still larger than I have told you.

The point is not merely that Torah is more powerful than nature, so powerful as to place limits on what Heaven can do. It is that the trivial *things* that concern Torah are important, even when they seem unimportant. Torah is not just for solving lofty problems.

The very topics about which the sages argue are given a kind of supernatural significance, even while, to the ordinary eye, they are trivial. There is a contrast between the results of the argument and the argument.

The argument is about something of no great consequence. But the results of the argument invoke the earth and Heaven.

The story says, beyond its own powerful message, that what sages discuss is of primary interest.

So the power of the sages is expressed by the claim that the little details of the law under dispute are important in Heaven and on earth. The sages disagree about small things because they agree on big ones. Cosmic meaning attaches to those small things *because* they are part of big ones.

Now what does Joshua mean when he rebukes Heaven and announces, "It is not in Heaven"?

In a passage inserted at just that point (which we did not read) Jeremiah, a Talmudic master, explains what Joshua means.

Jeremiah says, "Joshua means that the Torah has already been given at Mount Sinai. We pay no attention to an "echo" because You—that is, God—long ago wrote in the Torah at Mount Sinai, *"You must follow the majority"* (Ex. 23:2).

Jeremiah makes explicit something still more important, the power of the Torah as it is defined by a majority of the sages. We have already noticed that when the sages have to settle a dispute, they do so by voting.

They vote not because they are democratic, but because they believe that each of the sages bears Torah-learning of weight and significance. Sages vote because they have the wisdom to vote.

The point now is that when sages do vote, they take over the power of Heaven to reveal the Torah. God declared in the Torah that people should follow the majority of the sages or judges. God also is bound by the Torah, so God must follow the majority of the sages or judges.

Now this is parallel to Joshua's shout, "It is not in Heaven." But it improves what Joshua says, because it makes Joshua's general statement, that Torah is not in Heaven but is among the sages, into a more precise and

concrete saying.

By Jeremiah's explanation, Joshua is made to refer explicitly to the primacy of the sages' vote over all other forms of Heavenly instruction. The sages take the place of Heaven. Their vote binds *even* Heaven.

This is a strong claim of power. It is made in a world in which holy men and miracle-workers are everywhere. People believe in the supernatural power of miracle-workers.

That is true for the Jews as much as for anyone else. In the next story you will see the conflict between a wonder-worker, who is not a sage, and a sage. The sage will clearly believe in the power of the wonder-worker to perform miracles. At the same time, the sage will make his own claim. The sage will not admire or respect the wonder-worker's sort of miracle.

The sage claims a power nearly equal to that of Heaven. For what the sage knows is what Heaven knows. Torah binds Heaven. And, here on earth, the sage represents Torah and is himself a living Torah. The sage votes and decides what the Torah will be.

That is a tremendous claim, a grand vision.

Now keep in mind one last point: what is it that makes the sage into a sage? It is what the sage *knows*. By using one's mind and mastering Torah, one learns how to reason. By reasoning in Torah, the sage can take over what Heaven has given. By learning and reasoning, what Heaven has given—namely the Torah—becomes the property and the possession of human beings, of our sages of blessed memory.

It is remarkable to envision the power of the human mind to enter into the mysteries of Heaven and of earth. The sage takes over the power of Heaven and the rule over earth.

What a dream of humanity! What an exultation of our minds, of our power to think, to know, and to understand!

1. Why does the story seem complete without our knowing the topic of the dispute?

2. Do you think the storyteller made a mistake in not telling us about what the sages argued on that day? Do you think he cares? Is it important for the point he wishes to make?

3. Are there other details the storyteller has not told us? Do you think the story is weaker or less clear because we do not know how large the schoolhouse is? Who else was there?

4. What are some of the topics of Torah-learning that you have studied? Are the laws of keeping *kosher* always general, or are some of them about rather small things? Why are they all important?

5. How does Jeremiah make what Joshua says more concrete? Does Jeremiah refer to the practice of the sages of his own day? Under what circumstances do you think sages vote? What claim does Jeremiah make in behalf of their vote?

6. Why do sages have the power to shape the Torah through their vote?

7. What is the logic behind the position of Joshua and of Jeremiah, that Heaven accepts the authority of Torah? Why should Heaven be bound by the rules of the Torah?

8. Can you relate the idea that Heaven is bound by the rules of the Torah to the picture of God's rejoicing that "my children" have conquered me? Why should God be so happy? Do you think God is pleased that God's children—the sages—have mastered the Torah the way God wanted them to?

9. What are some of the other kinds of "holy men" or "miracle-workers" besides sages? Can you imagine what power other sorts of people would have claimed for themselves? What are the kinds of miracles people would have wanted these other kinds of "miracle-workers" to do? Do you think sages can do those other kinds of miracles?

10. Why should peoples' ability to think be so important in the minds of sages?

PART FIVE

How Do Sages Pray?

18. How Do Sages Pray?

When Yohanan ben Zakkai asked Vespasian for the right to go to Yavneh, one of the three things he wanted was to be able to establish a prayer house. So it is clear that sages believe in prayer, not only in Torah study, as a tie between Heaven and earth. We have to ask what sort of prayer they will want, and what sort they will think undignified.

We do not hear about *dignity* every day. Yet dignity is the centerpiece of an important story, which says how *not* to do things. We cannot understand the relationship of the sage to Heaven if we do not learn the meaning of the word *dignity*. The notion of dignity is the most important thing the sages should teach you.

By that notion I mean knowing who you are and what you are worth, having a respect for yourself. In addition, dignity means making sure that— so far as you can, with respect for other people—you convey respect *for yourself* to other people. This is part of what Hillel meant when he told the man that the whole Torah is summed up in the idea not to do to someone else what is hateful to yourself.

You have to respect yourself before you can treat others with respect. And that means you have to treat yourself as a valued person and act in such a way that others will know you value yourself. This is dignity.

Later, you will learn from the Mishnah, "Who is honored? The one who honors other people."

But prior to that notion is this one: Who is honored? One who honors himself or herself. Here, too, is a famous saying of Hillel's:

If I am not for myself, who will be for me?

But if I am only for myself, what am I?

And if not now, when?

Now let us come back to the sages and their sense of dignity, of who they are.

How do we know that the sages regard themselves as worthy, honored, and esteemed? We know it from the stories about Hillel and Shammai, about the origins of Eliezer, about Yohanan ben Zakkai and Vespasian, and, especially, about Joshua, Eliezer, and the heavenly "echo."

A person who can say to Heaven, "Who are you to interfere when we are arguing about matters of law?" is a person of surpassing dignity.

A person who today can face Heaven and say, "The Torah is not in Heaven. The Torah is on earth—and among us!" is a person who knows his or her own worth.

But the sense of self-worth contained in these sayings is not the same as self-importance. It is a sense of worth based on what the sage knows, which is Torah. It is based on who teaches us Torah, that is to say, Moses our rabbi, who received Torah from Heaven.

So the sage is not immodest when he knows his own worth. But he also is not a person who demeans or lowers himself, even before the evidence of nature—of streams that run backward and of trees that move hither and yon. He is not impressed by supernatural intervention or by miracles, because he knows the value of Torah, specifically *as he knows Torah*.

What does this have to do with prayer?

The connection is simple. A person will pray in a dignified way, if he or she knows and takes seriously the value of Torah.

There will be no groveling, no demanding, no pleasing. There will be a relationship to Heaven in which a person asks for what Heaven already has promised. It is a relationship of certainty and reliability.

The sage who prays does so with dignity before Heaven because the sage knows who he is and why he may speak with authority before Heaven.

Knowing Torah is a way to work out a relationship to Heaven. It is a relationship of mutual caring, of parties who know and understand one another. It is a relationship based on knowledge of what each party wants and expects of the other: *all of this is in Torah*. It is Torah, then, that makes prayer possible for sages.

When we go to the synagogue, we do not make things up as we go along. We open a prayer book, a *siddur*. We say prayers that we said last week and the week before, indeed, prayers that Jews have said for more than two thousand years.

Why these prayers and not others (except as extras)?

Because these are the prayers that our sages of blessed memory worked out for us. These are prayers that flow from their knowledge of Torah. These are prayers that establish a relationship of trust and mutual confidence between Israel and God. They do so because they are prayers made by sages based on their knowledge of Torah, which God gave.

At this point in meeting our sages, our task is somewhat different from

what it has been. Until now the stories we have studied have told about people whom the sages admire and respect. They are stories that set good examples for us. They are about people whom the story-telling sages admire and want us to copy.

But now we turn to a story about someone whom the sages do not regard as a sage. It is about a wonder-worker, and that wonder-worker has a different relationship with God from the sages' relationship. The purpose of the story is to make fun of the wonder-worker—in whom our sages believe.

In a way, this story is the opposite of the story about Eliezer, Joshua, and the wonders of nature. It shows us a choice, a different way of seeing things, from the way of Joshua and of the sages in general. That is why the story is interesting.

In order to understand what people are and do, you have to know what *they might have been*, what they might have done. Imagine the choices they had. Then you can understand the choices they made.

You can understand what they are and what they do because you can see what they choose not to be and not to do. That is the way of wisdom.

Here is a story about what sages might have been but did not wish to be. The main character is the wonder-worker, Honi, who is not a sage. You will now see why.

1. Why did Yohanan ben Zakkai think it important to get from Vespasian the right to continue to pray? Did prayer become more important after the destruction of the Temple than it was before that time? Why?

2. When people are said to be dignified, do you think they are

99

going to be stuffy? Is that a meaning of dignity? But what other way can you define the term?

3. Is there a relationship between the idea of dignity and the idea of "moral authority" that we considered earlier? Do you look up more to someone who respects himself or herself than to someone who does not? Do you listen, even when you do not have to, to the advice of someone who is dirty, degraded, unrefined, loud, or coarse?

4. What does it mean to "know who you are and what you are worth"? What is anyone "worth"? Why is this a basic question for someone who is growing up?

5. Why does Hillel say that if you are not for yourself, no one else will be for you? Why does he think it important that you not be only for yourself?

6. What is the connection between the idea that "Torah is not in Heaven" and the way in which sages will think it proper to pray? Why do Jews today say prayers that the sages created more than two thousand years ago?

7. What does it mean to "worship the Lord in the beauty of holiness," and "with reverence" or "with dignity"? Why are these ideas that pleased our sages of blessed memory?

8. Can you imagine other sorts of relationships to Heaven besides the relationship of the sages? What are other ways to pray besides the way we pray in the synagogue? Would it be just as good to make things up as you go along?

9. How will you recognize a story about someone who is not a sage? Which traits mark stories about someone who is a sage? Do the storytellers express respect for the sages about whom they tell the story? Do they let anyone in their stories speak disrespectfully to the sages who are the heroes of their stories?

10. Why is there a close connection between Torah-learning and prayer? Why is Torah-study not enough? Why do sages also believe they—and we—should pray? What is the purpose of prayer as we know it in the synagogue?

19. The Sage and the Wonder-Worker

HONI PRAYS FOR RAIN, AND SIMEON REBUKES HIM
Mishnah Ta'anit 3:8

This story is about a rain-maker, Honi the circle-drawer. It tells how one day he prayed for rain, and rain came. While this is the main point, the story tells us more.

The main character of this story, Honi, is called "the circle-drawer," because he draws a circle, stands in it, and then tells Heaven what to do. He will not leave the circle until Heaven complies.

Honi seems childish. Children often make extreme demands and issue threats. Adults know that most of what you demand you never get. Most of your threats are wasted breath, because you cannot carry them out. If you do, they boomerang.

Honi demands a miracle from Heaven. What makes the story important is that he *gets* the miracle. Yet, as you already know, the sages will not be impressed by that fact. They do not admire miracles. They have in mind a different sort of relationship with Heaven, a relationship of dignity and learning. So Honi does not really get his miracle. The story will make fun of him.

What is the message? A relationship of demands and threats is unpredictable. You cannot depend on it. You make demands because you are not sure of what you will get. You ask for everything and hope to get something. Honi gets nothing, too little, too much—and then does not want what he originally demanded!

In a relationship of learning, you know what you must do, and you know what you may hope for. That is a relationship of predictable exchange. You can trust and honor the other party of that relationship. You have confidence in the relationship and believe in the other party. It is not an encounter of demands and threats because these are not necessary. It is a relationship of caring and commitment, of duty and of love.

The story before us is deep because it portrays a miracle-worker as very powerful and silly. Honi does what he says and gets what he wants. The sage of the story, Simeon b. Shatah, who is supposed to have lived about 175

B.C.E., believes in Honi's power. He respects that power. He knows it works. But he does not admire it. He has in mind a different relationship to Heaven. He wants to exercise a different kind of power.

MISHNAH TA'ANIT 3:8

אָמְרוּ לוֹ לְחוֹנִי הַמְעַגֵּל:

They said to Honi, the circle-drawer,
"Pray for rain."
He said to them,
"Go and take in the clay ovens used for Passover.
"so that they do not soften [in the rain that is coming]."
He prayed, but it did not rain.
What did he do?
He drew a circle
and stood in the middle of it
and said before Him,
"Lord of the world! Your children have turned to me,
"for before You, I am like a member of the family.
"I swear by Your great name—
"I'm simply not moving from here
"until you take pity on your children!"
It began to rain drop by drop.
He said,
"This is not what I wanted,
"but rain for filling up cisterns, pits, and caverns."
It began to rain violently.
He said,
"This is not what I wanted,

הִתְפַּלֵּל שֶׁיֵּרְדוּ גְשָׁמִים.
אָמַר לָהֶם:
צְאוּ וְהַכְנִיסוּ תַנּוּרֵי פְסָחִים,

בִּשְׁבִיל שֶׁלֹּא יִמּוֹקוּ.

הִתְפַּלֵּל, וְלֹא יָרְדוּ גְשָׁמִים.
מֶה עָשָׂה?
עָג עוּגָה
וְעָמַד בְּתוֹכָהּ,
וְאָמַר לְפָנָיו:
„רִבּוֹנוֹ שֶׁלְעוֹלָם, בָּנֶיךָ
שָׂמוּ פְנֵיהֶם עָלַי,
שֶׁאֲנִי כְבֶן בַּיִת לְפָנֶיךָ.

נִשְׁבָּע אֲנִי בְּשִׁמְךָ הַגָּדוֹל
שֶׁאֵינִי זָז מִכָּאן,

עַד שֶׁתְּרַחֵם עַל בָּנֶיךָ".

הִתְחִילוּ הַגְּשָׁמִים מְנַטְּפִין.
אָמַר
לֹא כָךְ שָׁאַלְתִּי,
אֶלָּא גִשְׁמֵי בוֹרוֹת שִׁיחִין
וּמְעָרוֹת.
הִתְחִילוּ לֵירֵד בְּזַעַף.
אָמַר
לֹא כָךְ שָׁאַלְתִּי,

102

<table>
<tr>
<td>

"but rain of good will,
 blessing, and graciousness."
Now it rained the right way,
until Israelites had to flee
from Jerusalem up to the
 Temple Mount
because of the rain.
Now they came and said to
 him,
"Just as you prayed for it to
 rain,
"now pray for it to go away."
He said to them,
"Go, see whether the stone of
 the strayers is disappeared."
Simeon b. Shatah sent [a
 message] to him:
"If you were not Honi,
"I should decree a ban of
 excommunication against
 you.
"But what am I going to do to
 you?
"For you make demands
 before the Omnipresent
"So he does what you want,
"like a son who makes
 demands on his father
"so he does what he wants.
"Concerning you Scripture
 says,
*Let your father and your mother
 be glad,*
and let her that bore you rejoice
 (Prov. 23:25)."

</td>
<td dir="rtl">

אֶלָּא גִשְׁמֵי רָצוֹן,
בְּרָכָה וּנְדָבָה.
יָרְדוּ כְתִקָּנָן,
עַד שֶׁיָּצְאוּ יִשְׂרָאֵל
מִירוּשָׁלַיִם לְהַר הַבַּיִת

מִפְּנֵי הַגְּשָׁמִים.
בָּאוּ וְאָמְרוּ לוֹ

„כְּשֵׁם שֶׁהִתְפַּלַּלְתָּ עֲלֵיהֶם
שֶׁיֵּרְדוּ,
כָּךְ הִתְפַּלֵּל שֶׁיֵּלְכוּ לָהֶן".
אָמַר לָהֶן
:„צְאוּ וּרְאוּ, אִם נִמְחַת אֶבֶן
הַטּוֹעִים"
שָׁלַח לוֹ שִׁמְעוֹן בֶּן שָׁטָח:

אִלְמָלֵא חוֹנִי אַתָּה,
גּוֹזְרַנִי עָלֶיךָ נִדּוּי

אֲבָל מָה אֶעֱשֶׂה לָךְ.

שֶׁאַתָּה מִתְחַטֵּא לִפְנֵי הַמָּקוֹם

וְעוֹשֶׂה לָךְ רְצוֹנֶךָ
כְּבֵן שֶׁהוּא מִתְחַטֵּא עַל אָבִיו

וְעוֹשֶׂה לוֹ רְצוֹנוֹ.
עָלֶיךָ הַכָּתוּב אוֹמֵר:

יִשְׂמַח אָבִיךָ וְאִמֶּךָ

וְתָגֵל יוֹלַדְתֶּךָ".

</td>
</tr>
</table>

Vocabulary

Honi, the circle-drawer	חוֹנִי הַמְעַגֵּל	drop by drop	מְנַטְּפִין
pray	הִתְפַּלֵּל	I wanted	שָׁאַלְתִּי
rain	גְּשָׁמִים	cisterns	בּוֹרוֹת
go	צְאוּ	pits	שִׁיחִין
take in	הַכְנִיסוּ	caverns	מְעָרוֹת
clay oven	תַנּוּר	violently	בְּזַעַף
so that	שֶׁ...	good will	רָצוֹן
soften	יִמּוֹקוּ	blessing	בְּרָכָה
he drew	עָג	graciousness	נְדָבָה
circle	עוּגָה	the right way	כְּתִקְנָן
in the middle of it	בְּתוֹכָהּ	the Temple Mount	הַר הַבַּיִת
before Him	לְפָנָיו	just as	כְּשֵׁם
Lord of the world	רִבּוֹנוֹ שֶׁלָּעוֹלָם	[for the rain] to go away	שֶׁיֵּלְכוּ לָהֶן
[they] have turned	שָׂמוּ פְנֵיהֶם	the stone of the strayers	אֶבֶן הַטּוֹעִים
member of the family	בֶּן בַּיִת	disappeared	נִמְחַת
I swear	נִשְׁבָּע אָנִי	if you were not	אִלְמָלֵא ... אַתָּה
I'm simply not moving	אֵינִי זָז	I would decree	גּוֹזְרַנִי
until	עַד	a ban of excommunication	נִדּוּי
[you will] take pity	תְּרַחֵם	make demands	מִתְחַטֵּא
[the rain] began	הִתְחִילוּ	the Omnipresent	הַמָּקוֹם
		Scripture	הַכָּתוּב

20. How the Story Works

Every story we have studied is a story of conflict. None tells us merely what happened. In each story the narrative details— he went here, he did this, he said that—create drama and make a point. Everything is formed to teach us a lesson. The stories are about people who disagree with one another. The purpose of the storyteller is to tell us which side is right.

Had the story ended with Honi's making the rain come and then go, what message should we have gained? At first glance it would have been the tale of how a great miracle-worker made rain and then turned it off.

But then Simeon b. Shatah appears. The first thing you wonder is: "Who's he? Where did he come from?" But then you see that the upsetting entry of a new personality into the story also changes the story around. It becomes a story that shows how childish Honi is. But now you will see that even without Simeon, the story is about a foolish man, a baby.

What do you see in the first part of the story, which tells about Honi alone? Essentially, there are five distinct acts in the story. Each is worked out in a conversation. This is something we noticed elsewhere.

The second thing you see is that everything in the story is rather funny. The story tells what Honi could *not* do, not what he could. In some ways, it reminds us of Balaam, in whom people believed, and who also pretended he could do much more than he could deliver.

Let's go over the story as a whole and then talk about it scene by scene.

MISHNAH TA'ANIT 3:8

אָמְרוּ לוֹ לְחוֹנִי הַמְעַגֵּל: הִתְפַּלֵּל שֶׁיֵּרְדוּ גְשָׁמִים.
אָמַר לָהֶם: צְאוּ וְהַכְנִיסוּ תַנּוּרֵי פְסָחִים, בִּשְׁבִיל שֶׁלֹּא יִמּוֹקוּ.
הִתְפַּלֵּל, וְלֹא יָרְדוּ גְשָׁמִים. מֶה עָשָׂה? עָג עוּגָה וְעָמַד בְּתוֹכָהּ,
וְאָמַר לְפָנָיו: „רִבּוֹנוֹ שֶׁלְעוֹלָם, בָּנֶיךָ שָׂמוּ פְנֵיהֶם עָלַי, שֶׁאֲנִי כְבֶן
בַּיִת לְפָנֶיךָ. נִשְׁבָּע אֲנִי בְשִׁמְךָ הַגָּדוֹל שֶׁאֵינִי זָז מִכָּאן, עַד שֶׁתְּרַחֵם
עַל בָּנֶיךָ". הִתְחִילוּ הַגְּשָׁמִים מְנַטְּפִין. אָמַר: לֹא כָךְ שָׁאַלְתִּי, אֶלָּא

גִּשְׁמֵי בוֹרוֹת שִׁיחִין וּמְעָרוֹת. הִתְחִילוּ לֵירֵד בְּזַעַף. אָמַר: לֹא כָךְ שָׁאַלְתִּי, אֶלָּא גִּשְׁמֵי רָצוֹן, בְּרָכָה וּנְדָבָה. יָרְדוּ כְּתִקְנָן, עַד שֶׁיָּצְאוּ יִשְׂרָאֵל מִירוּשָׁלַיִם לְהַר הַבַּיִת מִפְּנֵי הַגְּשָׁמִים. בָּאוּ וְאָמְרוּ לוֹ: „כְּשֵׁם שֶׁהִתְפַּלַּלְתָּ עֲלֵיהֶם שֶׁיֵּרְדוּ, כָּךְ הִתְפַּלֵּל שֶׁיֵּלְכוּ לָהֶן". אָמַר „צְאוּ וּרְאוּ, אִם נִמְחַת אֶבֶן הַטּוֹעִים". שָׁלַח לוֹ שִׁמְעוֹן בֶּן שָׁטָח: אִלְמָלֵא חוֹנִי אַתָּה, גּוֹזְרַנִי עָלֶיךָ נִדּוּי. אֲבָל מָה אֶעֱשֶׂה לָךְ, שֶׁאַתָּה מִתְחַטֵּא לִפְנֵי הַמָּקוֹם וְעוֹשֶׂה לָךְ רְצוֹנְךָ כְּבֵן שֶׁהוּא מִתְחַטֵּא עַל אָבִיו וְעוֹשֶׂה לוֹ רְצוֹנוֹ. וְעָלֶיךָ הַכָּתוּב אוֹמֵר: יִשְׂמַח אָבִיךָ וְאִמֶּךָ יוֹלַדְתֶּךָ".

They said to Honi, the circle-drawer, "Pray for rain." He said to them, "Go and take in the clay ovens used for Passover, so that they do not soften [in the rain that is coming]." He prayed, but it did not rain. What did he do? He drew a circle and stood in the middle of it and said before Him, "Lord of the world! Your children have turned to me, for before You, I am like a member of the family. I swear by Your great name—I'm simply not moving from here until you take pity on your children!" It began to rain drop by drop. He said, "This is not what I wanted, but rain for filling up cisterns, pits, and caverns." It began to rain violently. He said, "This is not what I wanted, but rain of good will, blessing, and graciousness." Now it rained the right way, until Israelites had to flee from Jerusalem up to the Temple Mount because of the rain. Now they came and said to him, "Just as you prayed for it to rain, now pray for it to go away." He said to them, "Go, see whether the stone of the strayers is disappeared." Simeon b. Shatah sent [a message] to him, "If you were not Honi, I should decree a ban of excommunication against you. But what am I going to do to you? For you make demands before the Omnipresent so he does what you want, like a son who makes demands on his father so he does what he wants. Concerning you Scripture says, *Let your father and your mother be glad, and let her that bore you rejoice* (Prov.23:25)."

(Scene One) They come to Honi and say, "Pray for rain." He boasts: "Go take in the ovens so the clay will not soften in the rain—which I, Honi, will now bring down by my prayers."

What happens?

Nothing.

So much for the boast. Honi cannot pray better, more effectively, than anyone else. If I were Honi, I should be embarrassed.

(Scene Two) Honi draws a circle and stands in the middle. He reminds God that the Israelites are God's children. Then he underlines who he, Honi, is. He is more of a child of God than the others. How so? "Everyone knows that I am like a member of the family before you."

Honi swears that he, the child of the family, will punish the head of the family. How? By standing in one spot until the head of the family does what Honi demands!

That sometimes is how children get things, I suppose. But they get them not because they force their fathers or their mothers to do what they want. Taking oaths and standing in circles may work—but not the way people think they work.

It really is just a way of taking advantage of the fact that your father and mother love you. You can force them to do what you want them to because they want to.

But the better way for Honi did not work. So now he has to say he is a member of God's special family.

And what happens? God plays a joke on Honi: "It began to rain drop by drop."

(Scene Three) Honi complains that this is not the kind of rain that will move him outside of his circle. "This is not what I wanted!"

So God plays another joke on "baby" Honi. God gives so much rain that the rain threatens to wash everything away—like the rain of the Flood in the time of Noah.

(Scene Four) Honi complains again that this, too, is *not* the kind of rain he wanted. Now he gets what he wants.

(Scene Five) God's last joke on Honi is that God still makes it rain too much. The people who came to Honi to ask him to make it rain now come and tell him to make it stop raining.

Honi tries another boast: "Go see if a certain stone is under water." This is as if to say, "If the stone is now submerged, I'll turn off the rain."

What happens? Nothing.

Now the story ends. Honi leaves the action. This ending is extremely sudden. Honi now should *do* something else. How about stepping outside the circle and announcing that he thanks God for doing what he so childishly had demanded? Honi does nothing.

Why not? Because the point is clear.

The storyteller now makes a comment on the story. He needs no more evidence about Honi. Honi's true character and power, and God's opinion of Honi, are self-evident.

But the storyteller is too smart not to repeat in words the point he already has made in the actions and dialogues he has described. You might miss the point.

So now we meet Simeon b. Shatah, a leading sage in the time in which Honi is supposed to have lived. And what does Simeon say? He says pretty much *what Honi had said about himself.* But he draws conclusions from the facts.

He says that Honi is indeed special. If anyone else tried Honi's stunt, the sages would drive him away. But Honi is what he says he is: "a spoiled child in the heavenly household."

Then the storyteller concludes by citing a verse of Scripture that underlines the special, familial relationship between Honi and Heaven.

The storyteller tells you what he thinks about this kind of relationship. He does not have a high opinion of it. Honi may get what he wants—but not quite. He gets nothing, he gets too little, he gets too much. It would appear that Heaven is playing games with Honi.

This is not a dignified relationship. Just as Honi is supposed to know how to get his way with Heaven, Heaven is supposed to know how to give Honi what he wants. But Heaven does not give Honi what he wants, not at all. So how much can Honi really know? He is a child who thinks he can force his parents to do what he wants, but he really cannot force anyone to do anything.

But why bother to declare someone who is cute and selfish to be outside the circle of sages? It is not worth the trouble. Honi, after all, does get what

he deserves—more or less.

Once more we notice how little information the storyteller gives us. In fact, he tells us so little that he leaves out a suitable ending. The story does not come to a conclusion. It just stops with Honi's last boast. Why not tell us more? Because the point is obvious.

Honi boasted and did not really get what he wanted. Now he has boasted again. Do we need to be told another three-act saga of how the miracle-worker, in fact, is the toy and plaything of Heaven? Obviously not. The story stops because it has made its point.

At the beginning of this unit we talked about dignity. Dignity is the sense of self-respect that someone who knows Torah gains for himself or herself. At the end we see the opposite.

Sages do not want miracles to tell them what the Torah is. They do not want miracle-workers in their group. They admit that there *are* miracles. They respect the power of miracle-workers. But that is besides the point.

The point is that they approach Heaven with secure knowledge of Torah, which Heaven gave to Israel. So they are people with confidence in themselves. The reason is that they know who they are. They know the value of what they are.

They are masters of Torah. Torah is the guide to Heaven and to earth, to all creation.

In contrast, Honi is a child. He gets his way, but he has no dignity. He has no standing. And when he gets his way, it is not precisely what he has in mind. So Heaven plays jokes on Honi. But Heaven takes Joshua seriously, in the last story, even when he disagrees with the heavenly echo!

When in the previous story God says, "My children have conquered me," God says this happily. True, all creatures are God's children. But there are some children who can make themselves into something nearly equal to God. There are some who remain just kids. And there is a difference.

The hero of the story about Honi is Simeon. Stories about him relate that he was an important sage in his day—toward the beginning of the second century B.C.E. In this story, Simeon gets the last laugh. The verse of Scripture that the storyteller cites explains why. The verse of Proverbs says, "Give your father and mother cause for delight." So Simeon's message is that if you are as close to God as everyone believes, you should behave like a son, not a baby. Honi begs like a kid, but a kid should learn to grow up. Simeon says it is hard to teach a spoiled kid to behave. That is why he cites Proverbs. So Simeon is the hero.

1. Why do the stories always form around points of conflict or disagreement? What purpose is served by shaping stories around tense situations.

2. Do you find the story about Honi funny? Does the storyteller arrange things to make fun of Honi? What does the storyteller think of miracle-workers?

3. Why do you think the way to approach this story is to talk about dignity? What relevance does the idea of dignity have to what Honi does and says?

4. Why does the sage believe that he has dignity? What does it mean to have standing before Heaven? What is the basis for the dignity of the sage?

5. Do you think Honi is like Balaam? Read Numbers Chapters Twenty-two, Twenty-three, and Twenty-four, and see what things the two men have in common. Do you think that the storyteller has the model of Balaam in mind when

he tells the story of Honi? Is the resemblance as close as that between Jeremiah and Yohanan ben Zakkai? If not, then what are the points in common? Do you think the storyteller wants us to think of Balaam? Or do you think we are the ones who discover the parallel?

6. How many jokes does Heaven play on Honi? Is any one of them the climactic one? Or are they simply a series of repeated jokes?

7. What is a childish relationship to parents? What is a child's relationship to parents? What difference is there? When do you stop being a child to your parents? Is it possible to have a mature relationship to parents even when you are a child? Even when you are an adult, can you have a childish relationship to your parents?

8. Why do you think the sages regard the relationship of Honi to Heaven as childish? How would they explain that their relationship is different? Why is it different? What comment would Joshua make on this story about Honi?

9. Why does the storyteller not tell us what clothes Honi wore on the day he made the rain? What other details does he leave out? What details does he include, and why does he have to include them? Does it matter whether or not the story really happened?

10. Does a parent want children "to conquer"? What does it mean when a parent accepts the judgment of children and gives up his or her own opinion? Can you persuade your parents of your ideas? Do you always have to force them to listen to you? Why does Heaven listen to sages? Why do sages listen to Heaven?

PART SIX

Our Sages and Ourselves

21. The Humanity of Torah

Mishnah Abot 2:8

What do our sages do for us? They make the Torah into something human. Through our sages we can see Torah in flesh and blood.

Our sages take the words and make them live. The sage becomes a living Torah—so that the Torah may become like ourselves. Then we see how it works in the lives of ordinary human beings.

What makes Honi useless as a man of Torah is that he can do things other people cannot. He is not like us. So we cannot follow his model.

Honi is a miracle-worker. We are not. But, Simeon reminds us, we can grow up. Our relationship to God will be grown-up, dignified.

Joshua, Eliezer, Yohanan ben Zakkai, Hillel, and Shammai can be guides and models for us because they are not described as supernatural or as miracle-workers. They are people. True, they are unusual people. They have the power to learn and to take seriously what they learn. But we can master what they learn, because it is relevant to who we are and what we can become.

In our way, at our level, we have that same power. So we can strive to be a person like Hillel. We can learn his teachings and try to do them. He is a useful model for us. Honi is not.

Now what makes a person into a sage is learning of Torah. But if the learning of Torah is still not really natural to us, then the sage is just as special as Honi is special. If Torah-learning is not natural, we cannot imitate Hillel or Yohanan ben Zakkai or Joshua, because they are too made special—by what they know.

So the final question is, Is Torah for only a few people? Or is Torah something for every human being? And if it is for every human being, why is that so?

To answer that question in the way the sages answer it, we learn not a story but a saying. This is important, because most passages of Mishnah and Talmud are sayings, not stories. So you now learn how the great books of the sages work, how they say what they want to tell us.

For that purpose we take up the most important single saying in the name of Yohanan ben Zakkai.

It is important because it lays down the deepest belief about us held by our sages of blessed memory. It is that everyone is made to be a sage.

Sages see themselves not as special but as ordinary. Why? Because Torah is *about us.* Torah tells us what we really are—or can become, just as the sage provides us with a model of what we really are—or can become.

Now when you say, "really," you do not mean, the way I am just now. It is rather, *what I can be,* because of my basic character as a human being.

In a single word: Torah is God's design for us. Therefore when you learn Torah, you learn what you are made to learn, you do what you are made to do, you become what you really are.

That is the point in this saying.

MISHNAH ABOT 2:8

Rabban Yohanan ben Zakkai received [Torah] from Hillel and Shammai.	רַבָּן יוֹחָנָן בֶּן זַכַּאי קִבֵּל מֵהִלֵּל וּמִשַּׁמַּאי
He would say	הוּא הָיָה אוֹמֵר:
If you have learned much Torah	אִם לָמַדְתָּ תוֹרָה הַרְבֵּה,
do not think well of yourself [on that account]	אַל תַּחֲזִיק טוֹבָה לְעַצְמָךְ
for to that end were you created	כִּי לְכָךְ נוֹצָרְתָּ.

Vocabulary

received	קִבֵּל	for yourself	לְעַצְמָךְ
you learned	לָמַדְתָּ	because	כִּי
much	הַרְבֵּה	for this	לְכָךְ
do not	אַל	you were created	נוֹצָרְתָּ
claim	תַּחֲזִיק		

he form of what Yohanan claims is not difficult to grasp.

The saying is in three parts, but it is all one saying, just as many of the stories we have seen. But this one is much simpler in form, just three clauses.

Yohanan claims that we are made to learn Torah. Let us dwell on what he says and what it means. Then we can see very clearly why the stories about our sages are important.

Yohanan tells you something that you won't find surprising. He says, "If you've learned a lot of Torah, don't think you're something special—*because you were made to learn Torah.*"

You can't be especially proud to do what you're made to do. If you're a good athlete and can throw a ball into center field, why be proud of that? You're a good athlete. That's what you're supposed to do. It's natural. If you're a good swimmer and can swim the butterfly stroke, well, your body is strong enough to do it. There's nothing special about that. And so, too, if you're a good singer, or if you're a good student in school. We are what we are. We do what we are made to do. We do well what comes naturally.

Yohanan says this about *Torah.* What does he mean? He means that it's perfectly natural for everyone to learn *Torah,* because God made us into human beings who have eyes to see *Torah* and ears to hear *Torah* and minds to understand *Torah.* Why? Because what is *Torah,* if not what God tells us, and what God tells us is *truth.*

That is why, when we meet our sages, we meet people who show that it is natural to learn Torah. Through what they do and say, they act out Torah on the stage of real life.

But beyond these stories about our sages, there is a second, and better, way to meet our sages and so to learn Torah. And that is the way of studying the great books which our sages made.

In these books our sages teach not only by example but by reasoned sayings. In these sayings we have generalizations. That is, Mishnah and Talmud give us words that can speak of any kind of person living in any kind of world.

It is our work to take these teachings about things or people *in general*

117

and to turn them into stories *about ourselves.*

That is the main point: When we meet our sages, we meet ourselves—or, rather, ourselves as we can be. When we meet our sages, we meet Torah. *And Torah is about us.*

STORY STUDY SHEETS

These five sheets give copies of the stories in this book, Hebrew on one side and English on the other. You may find it helpful to clip out these sheets on the dotted line, so you can use them while working through the book.

BABYLONIAN TALMUD SHABBAT 31a

נָכְרִי אֶחָד בָּא לִפְנֵי שַׁמַּאי, אָמַר לוֹ: גַּיְירֵנִי
עַל מְנָת שֶׁתְּלַמְּדֵנִי כָּל הַתּוֹרָה כּוּלָהּ כְּשֶׁאֲנִי עוֹמֵד עַל רֶגֶל אַחַת.
דְּחָפוֹ בְּאַמַּת הַבִּנְיָן שֶׁבְּיָדוֹ. בָּא לִפְנֵי הִלֵּל, גַּיְירֵיהּ. אָמַר לוֹ:
דַּעֲלָךְ סְנֵי לְחַבְרָךְ לָא תַּעֲבֵיד — זוֹ הִיא כָּל הַתּוֹרָה כּוּלָהּ, וְאִידָךְ —
פֵּירוּשָׁהּ הוּא, זִיל גְּמוֹר.

HILLEL, SHAMMAI, AND THE PERSON WHO WANTED TO LEARN TORAH

. . . A certain gentile came before Shammai [and] said to him, "Convert me on condition that you teach me the whole Torah while I stand on one foot." He pushed him out with the builder's cubit which was in his hand. [When] he went before Hillel, he converted him [as] he said to him, "What is hateful to you, do not do to your neighbor. That is the whole Torah, and the rest is commentary; go and learn [it]."

מֶה הָיָה תְחִלָּתוֹ שֶׁל רַבִּי אֱלִיעֶזֶר בֶּן הוּרְקָנוֹס. בֶּן עֶשְׂרִים וּשְׁתַּיִם שָׁנָה הָיָה וְלֹא לָמַד תּוֹרָה. פַּעַם אַחַת אָמַר אֵלֵךְ וְאֶלְמוֹד תּוֹרָה לִפְנֵי רַבָּן יוֹחָנָן בֶּן זַכַּאי. אָ״ל אָבִיו הוּרְקָנוֹס אִי אַתָּה טוֹעֵם עַד שֶׁתַּחֲרוֹשׁ מְלֹא מַעֲנָה. הִשְׁכִּים וְחָרַשׁ מְלֹא מַעֲנָה. הָלַךְ וְיָשַׁב לוֹ לִפְנֵי רַבָּן יוֹחָנָן בֶּן זַכַּאי בִּירוּשָׁלַיִם עַד שֶׁיָּצָא רֵיחַ רַע מִפִּיו. אָמַר לוֹ רַבָּן יוֹחָנָן בֶּן זַכַּאי אֱלִיעֶזֶר בְּנִי כְּלוּם סָעַדְתָּ הַיּוֹם. שָׁתַק. שׁוּב אָמַר לוֹ וְשָׁתַק. שָׁלַח וְקָרָא לְאַכְסַנְיָא שֶׁלּוֹ אָ״ל כְּלוּם סָעַד אֱלִיעֶזֶר אֶצְלְכֶם. אָמְרוּ לוֹ אָמַרְנוּ שֶׁמָּא אֵצֶל רַבִּי הָיָה סוֹעֵד. אָמַר לָהֶם אַף אֲנִי אָמַרְתִּי שֶׁמָּא אֶצְלְכֶם הָיָה סוֹעֵד בֵּינִי וּבֵינֵיכֶם אָבַדְנוּ אֶת רַבִּי אֱלִיעֶזֶר מִן הָאֶמְצַע. אָ״ל כְּשֵׁם שֶׁיָּצָא לָךְ רֵיחַ רַע מִפִּיךְ כָּךְ יֵצֵא לָךְ שֵׁם טוֹב בַּתּוֹרָה.

ELIEZER BEN HYRCANUS GOES TO STUDY TORAH

What was the beginning of Rabbi Eliezer ben Hyrcanus? He was twenty-two years old and had not [yet] studied Torah. One time he said, "I will go and study Torah from Rabban Yohanan ben Zakkai." Said his father Hyrcanus to him, "You will not taste a thing before you plow the entire furrow." He rose early in the morning and plowed the entire furrow [and then went to Jerusalem]. He went and sat before Rabban Yohanan ben Zakkai in Jerusalem, until a bad breath came out of his mouth. Said Rabban Yohanan ben Zakkai to him, "Eliezer, my son, have you eaten at all today?" He was silent. [Rabban Yohanan ben Zakkai] asked him again. Again he was silent. [Rabban Yohanan ben Zakkai] sent for the owners of his hostel and asked them, "Did Eliezer have anything to eat in your place?" They replied, "We thought he would eat with you, Rabbi." He said to them, "And I thought he would eat with you! You and I, between us, [almost] destroyed Rabbi Eliezer." [Rabban Yohanan ben Zakkai] said to him, "Even as a bad breath came out of your mouth, so shall your fame go forth in Torah."

ABOT D'RABBI NATHAN CHAPTER FOUR

כְּשֶׁבָּא אַסְפַּסְיָינוּס לְהַחֲרִיב אֶת יְרוּשָׁלַיִם, אָמַר לָהֶם: שׁוֹטִים,
מִפְּנֵי מָה אַתֶּם מְבַקְשִׁים לְהַחֲרִיב אֶת הָעִיר הַזֹּאת וְאַתֶּם
מְבַקְשִׁים לִשְׂרוֹף אֶת בֵּית הַמִּקְדָּשׁ? וְכִי מָה אֲנִי מְבַקֵּשׁ מִכֶּם —
אֶלָּא שֶׁתְּשַׁגְּרוּ לִי קֶשֶׁת אַחַת אוֹ חֵץ אַחַת, וְאֵלֵךְ לִי מִכֶּם. אָמְרוּ לוֹ:
כְּשֵׁם שֶׁיָּצָאנוּ עַל שְׁנַיִם רִאשׁוֹנִים שֶׁהֵם לְפָנֶיךָ וַהֲרַגְנוּם, כָּךְ נֵצֵא
לְפָנֶיךָ וְנַהַרְגְךָ. כֵּיוָן שֶׁשָּׁמַע רַבָּן יוֹחָנָן בֶּן זַכַּאי, שָׁלַח וְקָרָא לְאַנְשֵׁי
יְרוּשָׁלַיִם וְאָמַר לָהֶם: בָּנַי, מִפְּנֵי מָה אַתֶּם מַחֲרִיבִין אֶת הָעִיר
הַזֹּאת, וְאַתֶּם מְבַקְשִׁים לִשְׂרוֹף אֶת בֵּית הַמִּקְדָּשׁ? וְכִי מַהוּ מְבַקֵּשׁ
מִכֶּם—הָא אֵינוֹ מְבַקֵּשׁ מִכֶּם אֶלָּא קֶשֶׁת אַחַת אוֹ חֵץ אַחַת, וְיֵלֵךְ לוֹ
מִכֶּם. אָמְרוּ לוֹ: כְּשֵׁם שֶׁיָּצָאנוּ עַל שְׁנַיִם שֶׁלְּפָנָיו וַהֲרַגְנוּם, כָּךְ
נֵצֵא עָלָיו וְנַהַרְגֵהוּ. הָיוּ לְאַסְפַּסְיָינוּס אֲנָשִׁים שְׁרוּיִין כְּנֶגֶד
חוֹמוֹתֶיהָ שֶׁל יְרוּשָׁלַיִם, וְכָל דָּבָר וְדָבָר שֶׁהָיוּ שׁוֹמְעִין הָיוּ כוֹתְבִין
עַל הַחֵצִי, וְזוֹרְקִין חוּץ לַחוֹמָה, לוֹמַר שֶׁרַבָּן יוֹחָנָן בֶּן זַכַּאי מֵאוֹהֲבֵי
קֵיסָר הוּא. וְכֵיוָן שֶׁאָמַר לָהֶם רַבָּן יוֹחָנָן בֶּן זַכַּאי יוֹם אֶחָד וּשְׁנַיִם
וּשְׁלֹשָׁה וְלֹא קִבְּלוּ מִמֶּנּוּ, שָׁלַח וְקָרָא לְתַלְמִידָיו, לְרַבִּי אֱלִיעֶזֶר
וְרַבִּי יְהוֹשֻׁעַ. אָמַר לָהֶם: בָּנַי, עִמְדוּ וְהוֹצִיאוּנִי מִכָּאן. עֲשׂוּ לִי אָרוֹן
וְאִישַׁן בְּתוֹכוֹ. רַבִּי אֱלִיעֶזֶר אָחַז בְּרֹאשׁוֹ, רַבִּי יְהוֹשֻׁעַ אָחַז בְּרַגְלָיו,
וְהָיוּ מוֹלִיכִין אוֹתוֹ עַד שְׁקִיעַת הַחַמָּה, עַד שֶׁהִגִּיעוּ אֵצֶל שַׁעֲרֵי
יְרוּשָׁלַיִם. אָמְרוּ לָהֶם הַשּׁוֹעֲרִים: מִי הוּא זֶה? אָמְרוּ לָהֶן: מֵת הוּא.
וְכִי אֵין אַתֶּם יוֹדְעִין שֶׁאֵין מְלִינִים אֶת הַמֵּת בִּירוּשָׁלַיִם? אָמְרוּ
לָהֶן: אִם מֵת הוּא, הוֹצִיאוּהוּ. וְהוֹצִיאוּהוּ וְהָיוּ מוֹלִיכִין אוֹתוֹ, עַד
שֶׁהִגִּיעוּ אֵצֶל אַסְפַּסְיָינוּס. פָּתְחוּ הָאָרוֹן וְעָמַד לְפָנָיו. אָמַר לוֹ:
אַתָּה הוּא רַבָּן יוֹחָנָן בֶּן זַכַּאי? שְׁאַל מָה אֶתֵּן לָךְ. אָמַר לוֹ: אֵינִי
מְבַקֵּשׁ מִמְּךָ אֶלָּא יַבְנֶה שֶׁאֵלֵךְ בָּהּ וְאֶשְׁנֶה בָּהּ לְתַלְמִידַי וְאֶקְבַּע בָּהּ
תְּפִלָּה, וְאֶעֱשֶׂה בָּהּ כָּל מִצְוֹת. אָמַר לוֹ: לֵךְ, וְכָל מַה שֶׁאַתָּה רוֹצֶה
לַעֲשׂוֹת עֲשֵׂה. אָמַר לוֹ: רְצוֹנְךָ שֶׁאוֹמַר לְפָנֶיךָ דָּבָר אֶחָד? אָמַר לוֹ:
הֲרֵי אַתְּ עוֹמֵד בְּמַלְכוּת. מִנַּיִן אַתָּה יוֹדֵעַ? אָמַר לוֹ: כָּךְ מָסוּר לָנוּ
שֶׁאֵין בֵּית הַמִּקְדָּשׁ נִמְסָר בְּיַד הֶדְיוֹט אֶלָּא בְּיַד מֶלֶךְ, שֶׁנֶּאֱמַר: וְנִקַּף
סִבְכֵי הַיַּעַר בַּבַּרְזֶל וְהַלְּבָנוֹן בְּאַדִּיר יִפּוֹל. אָמְרוּ: לֹא הָיָה יוֹם אֶחָד
שְׁנַיִם וּשְׁלֹשָׁה יָמִים, עַד שֶׁבָּא אֵלָיו דְּיוּפְלָא מֵעִירוֹ שֶׁמֵּת קֵיסָר,
וְנִמְנוּ עָלָיו לַעֲמוֹד בְּמַלְכוּת.

YOHANAN BEN ZAKKAI GOES TO VESPASIAN AND SAVES THE TORAH

When Vespasian came to destroy Jerusalem he said to the inhabitants, "Fools, why do you seek to destroy this city, and why do you seek to burn the Temple? For what do I ask of you but that you send me one bow or one arrow, and I shall leave you?" They said to him, "Even as we went forth against the first two who were here before thee and slew them, so shall we go forth against thee and slay thee." When Rabban Yohanan ben Zakkai heard this, he sent for the men of Jerusalem and said to them, "My children, why do you destroy this city, and why do you seek to burn the Temple? For what is it that he asks of you? He asks of you only one bow or one arrow, and he will go off from you." They said to him, "Even as we went forth against the two before him and slew them, so shall we go forth against him and slay him." Vespasian had men stationed near the walls of Jerusalem. Every word which they overheard they would write down, attach [the message] to an arrow and shoot it over the wall, saying that Rabban Yohanan ben Zakkai was one of the Emperor's supporters. Now, after Rabban Yohanan ben Zakkai had spoken to them one day, two days and three days, and they still would not listen to him, he sent for his disciples, for Rabbi Eliezer and Rabbi Joshua. "My sons," he said to them, "arise and take me out of here. Make a coffin for me that I might lie in it." Rabbi Eliezer took the head end of it, Rabbi Joshua took hold of the foot; and they began carrying him as the sun set, until they reached the gates of Jerusalem. "Who is this?" the gatekeepers demanded. "It's a dead man," they replied. "Do you not know that the dead may not be held overnight in Jerusalem?" "If it's a dead man," the gatekeepers said to them, "take him out." They continued carrying him until they reached Vespasian. They opened the coffin, and [Rabban Yohanan ben Zakkai] stood up before him. "Are you Rabban Yohanan ben Zakkai?" [Vespasian] inquired; "Tell me, what may I give you?" "I ask of you only Yavneh, where I might go and teach my disciples and there establish a prayer [house] and perform all the commandments." "Go," Vespasian said to him, "and whatever you wish to do, do." Said [Rabban Yohanan] to him, "By your leave, may I say something to you?" "Speak," [Vespasian] said to him. Said [Rabban Yohanan] to him, "Lo, you [already] stand as royalty." "How do you know this?" [Vespasian asked]. [Rabban Yohanan] replied, "This has been handed down to us, that the Temple will not be surrendered to a commoner, but to a king; as it is said, And he shall cut down the thickets of the forest with iron, and Lebanon shall fall by a mighty one" (Is. l0:34). It was said: No more than a day, or two or three days, passed before a pair of men reached him from his city [announcing] that the emperor was dead and that he had been elected to succeed as king.

בְּאוֹתוֹ הַיּוֹם הֵשִׁיב רַבִּי אֱלִיעֶזֶר כָּל תְּשׁוּבוֹת שֶׁבָּעוֹלָם
וְלֹא קִבְּלוּ הֵימֶנּוּ. אָמַר לָהֶם: אִם הֲלָכָה כְּמוֹתִי—חָרוּב זֶה יוֹכִיחַ!
נֶעֱקַר חָרוּב מִמְּקוֹמוֹ מֵאָה אַמָּה; אָמְרוּ לוֹ: אֵין מְבִיאִין רְאָיָה מִן
הֶחָרוּב. חָזַר וְאָמַר לָהֶם: אִם הֲלָכָה כְּמוֹתִי—אַמַּת הַמַּיִם יוֹכִיחוּ!
חָזְרוּ אַמַּת הַמַּיִם לַאֲחוֹרֵיהֶם; אָמְרוּ לוֹ: אֵין מְבִיאִין רְאָיָה מֵאַמַּת
הַמָּיִם. חָזַר וְאָמַר לָהֶם: אִם הֲלָכָה כְּמוֹתִי—כָּתְלֵי בֵּית הַמִּדְרָשׁ
יוֹכִיחוּ! הִטּוּ כָּתְלֵי בֵּית הַמִּדְרָשׁ לִפֹּל; גָּעַר בָּהֶם רַבִּי יְהוֹשֻׁעַ, אָמַר
לָהֶם: אִם תַּלְמִידֵי חֲכָמִים מְנַצְּחִים זֶה אֶת זֶה בַּהֲלָכָה—אַתֶּם מַה
טִּיבְכֶם! לֹא נָפְלוּ מִפְּנֵי כְּבוֹדוֹ שֶׁל רַבִּי יְהוֹשֻׁעַ, וְלֹא זָקְפוּ מִפְּנֵי
כְּבוֹדוֹ שֶׁל רַבִּי אֱלִיעֶזֶר, וַעֲדַיִן מַטִּין וְעוֹמְדִין. חָזַר וְאָמַר לָהֶם: אִם
הֲלָכָה כְּמוֹתִי—מִן הַשָּׁמַיִם יוֹכִיחוּ! יָצְאתָה בַּת קוֹל וְאָמְרָה:
מַה לָּכֶם אֵצֶל רַבִּי אֱלִיעֶזֶר, שֶׁהֲלָכָה כְּמוֹתוֹ בְּכָל מָקוֹם. עָמַד רַבִּי
יְהוֹשֻׁעַ עַל רַגְלָיו וְאָמַר: לֹא בַּשָּׁמַיִם הִוא! אַשְׁכְּחֵיהּ רַבִּי נָתָן
לְאֵלִיָּהוּ, אָמַר לֵיהּ: מַאי עֲבֵד קֻדְשָׁא בְּרִיךְ הוּא בְּהַהִיא שַׁעְתָּא?
אָמַר לֵיהּ, קָא חָיֵיךְ וְאָמַר: נִצְּחוּנִי בָּנַי, נִצְּחוּנִי בָּנַי.

ELIEZER AND JOSHUA DEBATE AN ISSUE OF TORAH, AND HEAVEN IS ASKED TO JOIN THE DISCUSSION

On that day R. Eliezer brought forward all of the arguments in the world, but they did not accept [them] from him. Said he to them, "If the law agrees with me, let this carob-tree prove it." The carob-tree was torn a hundred cubits out of its place. They said to him, "No proof can be brought from a carob-tree." He said to them, "If the law agrees with me, let the stream of water prove it." The stream of water flowed backwards. They said to him, "No proof can be brought from a stream of water." Again he said to them, "If the law agrees with me, let the walls of the schoolhouse prove it." The walls inclined to fall. R. Joshua rebuked them, saying, "When disciples of sages are engaged in a legal dispute, what is your value?" Hence they did not fall, in honor of R. Joshua, nor did they resume the upright, in honor of R. Eliezer. [And they still are standing thus inclined.] Again he said to them, "If the law agrees with me, let it be proved from Heaven." An echo went forth and said, "Why do you dispute with R. Eliezer, for in all matters the law agrees with him!" But R. Joshua arose and exclaimed, "*It is not in heaven* (Deut. 30:12)." R. Nathan met Elijah and asked him, "What did the Holy One, blessed be He, do at that time?" He replied, "He laughed [with joy], saying, 'My sons have defeated Me. My sons have defeated me.' "

MISHNAH TA'ANIT 3:8

אָמְרוּ לוֹ לְחוֹנִי הַמְעַגֵּל: הִתְפַּלֵּל שֶׁיֵּרְדוּ גְשָׁמִים.
אָמַר לָהֶם: צְאוּ וְהַכְנִיסוּ תַּנּוּרֵי פְסָחִים, בִּשְׁבִיל שֶׁלֹּא יִמּוֹקוּ.
הִתְפַּלֵּל, וְלֹא יָרְדוּ גְשָׁמִים. מֶה עָשָׂה? עָג עוּגָה וְעָמַד בְּתוֹכָהּ,
וְאָמַר לְפָנָיו: „רִבּוֹנוֹ שֶׁלָּעוֹלָם, בָּנֶיךָ שָׂמוּ פְנֵיהֶם עָלַי, שֶׁאֲנִי כְבֶן
בַּיִת לְפָנֶיךָ. נִשְׁבָּע אֲנִי בְשִׁמְךָ הַגָּדוֹל שֶׁאֵינִי זָז מִכָּאן, עַד שֶׁתְּרַחֵם
עַל בָּנֶיךָ". הִתְחִילוּ הַגְּשָׁמִים מְנַטְּפִין. אָמַר: לֹא כָךְ שָׁאַלְתִּי, אֶלָּא
גִשְׁמֵי בוֹרוֹת שִׁיחִין וּמְעָרוֹת. הִתְחִילוּ לֵירֵד בְּזַעַף. אָמַר: לֹא כָךְ
שָׁאַלְתִּי, אֶלָּא גִשְׁמֵי רָצוֹן, בְּרָכָה וּנְדָבָה. יָרְדוּ כְתִקְנָן, עַד שֶׁיָּצְאוּ
יִשְׂרָאֵל מִירוּשָׁלַיִם לְהַר הַבַּיִת מִפְּנֵי הַגְּשָׁמִים. בָּאוּ וְאָמְרוּ לוֹ:
„כְּשֵׁם שֶׁהִתְפַּלַּלְתָּ עֲלֵיהֶם שֶׁיֵּרְדוּ, כָּךְ הִתְפַּלֵּל שֶׁיֵּלְכוּ לָהֶן". אָמַר
„צְאוּ וּרְאוּ, אִם נִמְחָת אֶבֶן הַטּוֹעִים". שָׁלַח לוֹ שִׁמְעוֹן בֶּן שָׁטַח:
אִלְמָלֵא חוֹנִי אַתָּה, גּוֹזְרַנִי עָלֶיךָ נִדּוּי. אֲבָל מָה אֶעֱשֶׂה לָךְ, שֶׁאַתָּה
מִתְחַטֵּא לִפְנֵי הַמָּקוֹם וְעוֹשֶׂה לָךְ רְצוֹנָךְ כְּבֵן שֶׁהוּא מִתְחַטֵּא עַל
אָבִיו וְעוֹשֶׂה לוֹ רְצוֹנוֹ. וְעָלֶיךָ הַכָּתוּב אוֹמֵר: יִשְׂמַח אָבִיךָ וְאִמֶּךָ
יוֹלַדְתֶּךָ".

HONI PRAYS FOR RAIN, AND SIMEON REBUKES HIM

They said to Honi, the circle-drawer, "Pray for rain." He said to them, "Go and take in the clay ovens used for Passover, so that they do not soften [in the rain that is coming]." He prayed, but it did not rain. What did he do? He drew a circle and stood in the middle of it and said before Him, "Lord of the world! Your children have turned to me, for before You, I am like a member of the family. I swear by Your great name—I'm simply not moving from here until you take pity on your children!" It began to rain drop by drop. He said, "This is not what I wanted, but rain for filling up cisterns, pits, and caverns." It began to rain violently. He said, "This is not what I wanted, but rain of good will, blessing, and graciousness." Now it rained the right way, until Israelites had to flee from Jerusalem up to the Temple Mount because of the rain. Now they came and said to him, "Just as you prayed for it to rain, now pray for it to go away." He said to them, "Go, see whether the stone of the strayers is disappeared." Simeon b. Shatah sent [a message] to him, "If you were not Honi, I should decree a ban of excommunication against you. But what am I going to do to you? For you make demands before the Omnipresent so he does what you want, like a son who makes demands on his father so he does what he wants. Concerning you Scripture says, *Let your father and your mother be glad, and let her that bore you rejoice* (Prov.23:25)."